Eric Oduro Wiafe

Towards a New Consciousness for a Better Africa: Some Topical Issues in Ghana

Table of Contents

Dedication

Dedicated to:

Mr. & Mrs. Annie Galea and family, Mr. Angelo Xuereb, Mr. Mario Vella, Ms. Miriam Gatt and Family, Msgr. Philip Calleja, Fr. Michael Xuereb and Family, Mr. Joseph Attard, Doreen Carabott and family and all my Maltese friends for their love and care.

Acknowledgements

I am grateful to God for His continuous love and care for me in spite of my unworthiness before Him, and also for the inspirations and courage He gives me to put down my thoughts on paper.

My gratitude goes to Rev. Fr. Samuel Korkordi for reading through the script and drawing my attention to some grammatical and typographical errors; and to all who give me support and encouragement in this endeavor to write.

I thank you all and wish you God's richest blessings.

Prologue

During my sojourn in Germany, I tried to engage in frank discussions with people from other African countries about their respective countries. I also read and watched reports from other African countries. It was just amazing to know the beauty and the potentialities of the African continent and the prospect to lift its people from the crutches of poverty, diseases and hardship.

It is true that some countries on the continent of Africa are experiencing hardships due to wars and brutalities, diseases and poverty, and of course bad leadership, but these situations should let the people sit up and do something positively to better their lot. The natural and human resources are so huge that when there is one mindedness everyone will have even more than enough for his or her life for many years to come. Greed, avarice, self-centeredness tell us that we do not have enough so we should scramble for the resources and think of only ourselves and our families. In the long run many people die or get maimed as a result of these wars and there is no peace for one to live and think of how to develop technologically to control nature. We keep on doing the old things in the same old ways and have to accept whatever we get from the developed countries. The hardship we go through should teach us a lesson to work for peace, love and unity while encouraging the youth to be innovative in order to change the destiny of Africa.

In these essays I tried to bring out few topics that we can consider for a better Africa. Many of the examples are coming from my home country Ghana; however, other African countries are cited as well.

In the first chapter I introduced my home country Ghana as one of many African countries that are making some headway in development. Interestingly, some people describe Africa as one big country. Well, this is the hope of many Africans that Africa with 54 Independent countries and many ethnic groupings and languages, will one day unite as one United Africa. This may take some time but there is hope for this kind of unity. The intention to write about Ghana is to point out that Ghana offers hope for Africa as she is working hard to strengthen her democratic credentials and giving quality life to her people. She has thus become a shining example to many African countries. This is a clear sign that with unity of purpose something good can be achieved in other African countries as well.

In the Second Chapter I discussed Information and Communication Technology (ICT) and how they can be used to propel Ghana and for that matter Africa's development. In an age of information and communication technology, to ignore ICT would be suicidal for any country.

I discussed also the symbolism of water in Africa in the third Chapter. This is a topic which looks at the important role water plays in the context of African traditional sense, but goes on to encourage the proper harnessing and management of water resource and making potable water accessible and affordable to the people.

The fourth Chapter is about the role that the media can play in Ghana's development. The Media is said to be the third estate of the realm. In other words, apart from the executive, parliamentary and judicious arms of government, the media comes next and it forms public opinion and can unite the people for action. So I looked at the role that the media can play in helping the society to work towards unity and advancement, and not only be a money making institution or a means to advance one's own interest but must look at issues objectively and promote Africa's development.

The making of a new Ghana forms the next chapter. I looked at what can be done to make Ghana a better nation. Some of the points raised here are also good for other African countries. We need to work assiduously to lift our countries from their doldrums of poverty and hardship.

For all the suggestions given in the previous chapters to materialize we need good leadership. This would come about when the youth are given the requisite training, trust, confidence and imbibed with a sense of nationalism. They would work hard to bring a change to Africa, so that Africa will be what the Akans of Ghana say "kra be hwe", meaning, making people yearn to come back and experience the excellence chalked by Africa.

I concluded with a poem which I dedicate to my Archbishop, Charles Palmer-Buckle and all people fighting for a better Africa.

Chapter One

1.0 Life in Ghana

1.1 Introduction

The African continent has received notoriety in the Western World as a continent ravaged by poverty, civil strives and diseases like HIV/AIDS. The presence of all these devastating phenomena paints a gloomy picture of the continent and thus hampers her development and progress. This is because such description of Africa does not encourage tourism and foreign investment, which are key areas that can shape the progress of any developing nation. It is therefore not a surprise when The Economist in its May 13-19, 2000 edition carried on its front page the caption: "Africa, the Hopeless Continent?" We know from the experience of people who have come

1

for the first time to certain countries in Africa, going back to their home countries with positive impressions and do come back again to meet with their new friends and families.

In this work about the life in Ghana, we would like to give the other side of the life on the continent using Ghana as a model country. We would give a short introduction to the country and then look at the life here from the political, religious, education, marriage and family, the economy and Ghanaian values. These areas will give us a bird's eye view of Ghana and in some ways Africa in general.

1.2 Short History

Ghana is in the West coast of Africa. She prides herself as the first African country, South of the Sahara, to gain political independence from the British on 6th March 1957 and became a Republic in 1960. It was previously called the Gold Coast because of the abundance of gold found there by the early explorers. The name Gold Coast was given by these explorers. The name Ghana was given by the founding fathers, especially by Dr. J. B. Danquah and Dr. Kwame Nkrumah, because of the historical and cultural similarities and relationship found between the Old Ghana Empire and the present day Ghana. The name is of a royal decent and significant in meaning for the people. As royals they turn to lead in many aspects of the life of Africans by charting a path of peace, unity and good governance for the entire continent.

1.3 Political Life

Ghana is a democratic state. After her independence in 1957, it has gone through many difficult times due to political instabilities. The nation experienced a stable form of government from 1981 but since 1992 there has been in vogue a new democratic dispensation characterized by peaceful handing over to successive governments. This means that the people believe now of the power of election so that they can choose their leaders to run the affairs of the nation. As stated above, hitherto there were military adventurisms, which to many Ghanaians retarded the development of the nation.

There is also a certain awareness of the citizenry of their fundamental human rights, which they uphold with conviction and dignity. It is also interesting to see many Ghanaians, young and old discussing political issues and contributing through phone-in programmes on Fm radio stations to issues at state in the nation. We see the desire and efforts of Ghanaians to make democracy work so that Ghana would continue to be a model of democracy to other African nations.

1.4 Religious Life

On the religious life of Ghanaians, it is important to state that Ghanaians are very much religious in nature. The religiosity of Ghanaians is based on their traditional upbringing. They grow up imbibed with the religion of the people. From pregnancy to death, there are rituals performed at every stage of one's life. We can talk about actions and prohibitions of the pregnant woman, out-dooring and naming ceremonies, marriage and death. Libations are poured and sometimes sacrifices are made to the deities and ancestors of one's traditional home for blessings and to remove curse. There is also the belief in witchcraft, which even the most educated people have been influenced into believing in its existence. The theme of witchcraft feature very much in the preaching of some pastors. There exist in Ghana also witchcraft colonies, especially in the northern part of Ghana. It is a belief which is difficult for the people to shed off. During festivals and funerals one comes face to face with many of the traditional beliefs and practices of the people. It is expected that everyone in spite of one's new belief, participates in the ceremonies of his or her people. This poses a challenge to Christians.

Christianity and Islam have made inroads into the life of Ghanaians. The Northern part of Ghana is predominantly Islam and the Southern part is

Christianity. Due to migration such demographical distributions are affected.

Ghana is predominantly Christian and this could be found in the cities, towns and villages, but Islam, which mainly found in the northern part of Ghana is also making inroads into the cities and towns. Today, Islam provides also educational and health opportunities to Moslems and also the general public. There is much support for their projects from some Islamic countries like Saudi Arabia and Iran.

The percentage distributions of the various religions from the 2000 census of Ghana are as follows:

Christianity	...	69%
African Traditional Religion	...	8.5%
Islam	...	15.6%
Others	...	6.9 %

Christianity is growing by leaps and bounds. We have the mainline Churches, the Charismatic and then the Pentecostals. It is important to state that the Charismatic Churches are making lots of inroads into the Ghanaian society due to the fact that they are making very good use of the media, especially Radio and Television. They are also emphasizing on wealth creation and the elimination of poverty in their lives. Since majority of the people are poor such messages are very appealing. Many young men and women want to break the chain of poverty and attain some level of dignity in their lives and they think the new Charismatic Churches are the place for the realization of their expectations. But there is the need for caution here since riches are not like manna falling from heaven. They should do more to inculcate into the people striving for a certain level of education, good use of one's skill or talent, hardwork, proper and lawful acquisition of wealth and patience as one strives to weather the storm of life in order to make it in life. Since the target group is the tertiary students core human values should be taught to the students so that they can impact on the society.

The orthodox Churches form the young people at the basic and secondary levels and they lose them to the new Churches at the tertiary level. It is therefore important that the orthodox Churches redouble their efforts in the call for new evangelization, otherwise they will continue losing a lot of their members and their future to the new Churches.

The general trend in the celebrations of almost all the Churches is that of a lively singing and dancing. This is the African way of worshipping. It is therefore not surprising that the orthodox Churches have adapted such ways of worship in their liturgy. This is what attracts the youth to the Church. It is in this light that we can say that the Charismatic Renewal Movement in the orthodox Churches in Ghana has been a blessing since it answers most of the needs of orthodox Christians who go to the new emerging Churches for an African spiritual satisfaction.

In Ghana, the Churches are always full to capacity on Sundays. The normal life of most Ghanaians, including the youth is Family, Work and Church. The Churches have many societies. For instance, the Catholic Church has many societies which are never short of members. They have their uniforms and these are worn on special occasions like feast days of the society or the parish. They offer spiritual, material and social support to the members. They pay dues for the running of the society and also for the support of their programmes. They support their members during funerals and marriage ceremonies. They also organize themselves to raise funds to support their parishes and stations. Furthermore, they support their priests by bringing offertories during Church services. Some of the groups in the Catholic Church are Knights and Ladies of Marshall, Knights and Ladies of St. John International, Catholic Youth Organization (CYO), Catholic Organization for Social and Religious Advancement (COSRA), Young Christian Workers (YCW), Knights and Ladies of the Altar, Saint Theresa of the Child Jesus Society, Christian Mothers Association, Catholic Women Association and Catholic Men Association.

1.5 Education

It is important to state that majority of the people in Ghana live in the rural areas. The figure is about 70%. The illiteracy rate therefore is high. There is an effort by the government and the people of Ghana to raise the literacy rate since education is the bedrock of development.

The Schools in the towns and cities are better equipped and organized than that of the rural areas, but even here some of the schools have poor and inadequate infrastructure namely, classrooms and accommodation facilities for teachers. There are also inadequate school materials like furniture, books, pencils and pen. In the rural areas there are some schools, which have dilapidated infrastructure, and some even do not have befitting place to hold classes and so have to hold their classes under trees. In such cases when it rains it is a holiday for the students. The situation is so appalling but despite the fact that the government promises to do something about it the situation remains the same. It is a huge task but if education is the future of the people and the nation, then much of the nation's revenue should be invested in it since the benefit will be tremendous.

The pupils and students from the kindergarten to the Secondary schools wear common uniforms. It is in the tertiary institutions that people are at liberty to wear what they like. But the dressing of some of the female students sometimes create conflict as some Christian students who see it as immoral but other students see it as a demonstration of freedom and human rights.

Due to the challenging economic and social conditions in Ghana and the world at large many parents try to give their children the best of education, for this reason they look for part-time teachers for their children. It is not an easy task for the children to learn at school and do part-time at home, but to make it in life one must learn very hard and pass examinations so as to go to the university and end up with a good job.

Many of those who do not make it in education end up as street children. Some of the young people come from the rural areas to the cities to look for some prospects in their life but end up also as street children thus falling into some of the problems of streetism, namely drug addiction, armed robbery and prostitution.

1.6 Marriage and Family

Marriage is seen as a noble institution and for the Ghanaian and African marriage is not only between the man and the woman but also between the two respective families of the couple. So the whole families are involved in the marriage preparations from its beginning to the end. They make sure that the two people about to be married come from good homes without any genetic problems like diseases and lunacy. They also make sure that there are no kleptomaniacs in the families of the prospective couples. When the families have ascertained the worthiness of the marriage, they proceed with the necessary arrangements and rituals to certify and solidify the marriage. Just as it takes the two families to tie the knot of marriage, when it comes to divorce the families are also involved. But they try as much as they can to protect the marriage and it is when nothing else could be done to sustain the marriage that they allow for divorce.

The Ghanaian loves children and so abhors barrenness and impotence. There is always a problem in the marriage if the woman cannot bring forth a child. But many forget that the problem could also emanate from the man. The problem of barrenness sometimes leads to separation of the couple and the worse case is divorce. This is because children are seen as those to continue with the ancestral lineage and not to have them is to bring the lineage to extinction. The love for children is a big hindrance to the family planning programme which is aimed at fighting poverty. It is mainly the educated ones who are practicing family planning. The law in Ghana permits monogamy but it is important to state that Muslims and Traditional people practise the polygamous system of marriage.

Ghanaians practise the extended family system. This means that the family is not only that of the father, mother and the children but also that of the grandparents, uncles, nephews, nieces, etc. The extensive nature of the family also calls for the support of each member in every situation of life. At the family home the people even eat together in one bowl as a sign of unity, love and peace.

In the traditional family system, the training of each child is the responsibility of every member of the family. On the naming, marriage or funeral of a member of the family, it is incumbent that all members of the family is present at the celebrations and to absent oneself is to alienate oneself from the family, which in this context is suicidal.

It is important to point out that there are so many influences on the Ghanaian traditional family system. There is the trend in the cities to emphasize the nucleus family system as against the extended family system due to westernization and urbanization. But this influence is difficult to penetrate the traditional institution since the external family system is so strong in Ghana and Africa.

1.7 Economics

Ghana, as already stated, is a developing country. The poverty level is high and the people feel it deep in their hearts and lives. Good and proper housing is big problem in Ghana. Some young people sleep outside on the streets and so are at the mercy of the weather.

There are many people who because of their meager salaries cannot afford three square meals a day. This is because their salaries cannot meet their expenditure because food is expensive and they have to take care of their other family commitments.

As already stated, education in Ghana and Africa for that matter is expensive and not many people have access to it. In other words, poverty prevents many young people access to good education, especially at the higher level. The government has introduced the Free Compulsory Universal Basic Education (FCUBE) but this is yet to be translated into practical life of the people.

The Ghanaian is highly gifted, hardworking and committed to noble values. The country has a lot of potentials. She is endowed with natural resources and the gift of hope for better things to come in the future. What she needs is good leadership that can turn the fortunes of Ghana to prosperity.

One significant thing about the Ghanaian is that in spite of the problems and economic hardships he or she is always filled with joy and happiness. The Ghanaian does not allow poverty to defeat his or her happiness. So one can still see children playing with joy, adults also going about their activities with joy and happiness and sharing the little they have with others who may be of need of it, especially family members.

1.8 The Ghanaian Values

The life of the Ghanaian is characterized by the fear of God. Many of the values of the Ghanaian are based on their belief in God, who was known before the arrival of Christianity. The Ghanaian cherishes the values of respect to elders, old age and people in authority.

The other value is hospitality. There is always a talk about the Ghanaian hospitality. Archbishop (Emeritus) Kwasi Sarpong gives the reason for this when he said, "The abhorrence of disgrace may well be the underlying rationale for the Ghanaian's sense of generosity, especially to strangers. He may not like a tribe and its members, but this will never prevent him from treating with kindness a guest from that tribe." (Peter Kwasi Sarpong, 1974, p.66). To be hospitable is a duty for every Ghanaian. There is a saying that, "The stranger does not sleep in the street" or "One need not be begged to eat" (Peter Sarpong, 1974, p. 66).

The Ghanaian has also a sense of gratitude and this is expressed in everyday life situations as we hear people saying, "Medaase", which in Akan means, "Thanks you" to a good act done to someone.

1.9 Conclusion

In conclusion, we can say that Ghana, just like any African country is a beautiful country. It is rich in tradition and culture. Ghana has lively people who are hospitable and reachable. The people live their life in hope of the future believing in the guidance and protection of God who provides for their daily needs. It is my hope that people from other parts of the world will come to experience this life of the Ghanaian and participate in their family life, festivals and Church or Islamic services feasts for a deepening of friendship and solidarity among peoples of other races and faiths.

Chapter Two

2.0 Making Information and Communication Technology (ICTs) a factor for change in Developing Nations: A Case of Ghana

2.1 Introduction

The use of Information and Communication Technologies (ICTs) is transforming and accelerating the growth of many nations of the world in all aspects of life: political, economic, social and educational. ICTs have become so important to development that when a nation and her people do not make use of such modern means of communication that nation is going to lurk behind in development. In this paper, I wish to look at how ICTs can transform developing nations with special reference to Ghana. In treating this topic I will give a definition of the basic terms that are used in the discussion, the problems that confront Ghana which militate against her development will be discussed so as to substantiate the need for change; I will then look at what ICTs can do in effecting change to

15

bring about rapid development; the possible challenges that are to be envisaged and how to overcome them; the recommendations and conclusion will then follow.

2.2 Definition of Terms

a. *Information and Communication Technology (ICT)*

In explaining what ICT is all about, Cheung (2001) quotes Hamelink as saying that, 'ICT encompass all those technologies that enable the handling of information and facilitate different forms of communication among human actors, between human beings and electronic systems, and among electronic systems.' He went on to say that this definition entails two parts: 'technology' and 'information and communication'. Technology according to Cheung (2001) is the means to serve the goals of information handling and communication.

b. *Information*

Information, according to the Merriam-Webster Online Dictionary is "knowledge obtained from investigation, study, or instruction." I must say that here we can also add one's experience, since as the saying goes "Experience is the best teacher."

c. *Communication*
Communication is defined as a process by which information is exchanged between individuals through a common system of symbols, signs, or behavior.

d. *Development*
Development is the act, process or result of developing. It is also the determination of the best techniques for applying a new device or processes to production of goods and services. Both definitions fit the context within which I am about to discuss the concept of development in Ghana.

f. *Change*
To change is to give a completely different form or appearance to; transform. In this essay what I mean by change is more of transformation from the situation that Ghanaians find themselves to a much better one.

2.3 Why the need for Change?

Ghana is one of the developing countries of the world. In March 2001 Ghana entered into the Heavily Indebted Poor Countries (HIPC) Initiative which was launched by the International Monetary Fund (IMF) and the World Bank in September 1996. She reached the completion point of the initiative on the 15th of July 2004. The reason for such an initiative was to seek for debt relief to reduce poverty in Ghana. A Ghanaian Times Reporter quoted a World Bank report on Ghana as stating that, "Ghana is one of the few countries in Africa that have carried out programmes to lift a significant percentage of their citizens above the poverty line, and is likely to meet Millennium Development Goals (MDG) target of halving poverty by 2010." We can say that on paper the government would claim to have made some gains in alleviating the poverty of the people but in reality majority of the people still wallow in abject poverty.

We can take some few indicators of poverty status in Ghana:

i.   Education: There is a high illiteracy rate in Ghana. Even though there is the Free Compulsory Basic Education and also the introduction of the Government feeding programme there are still many people who do not go to school. There are also many drop-outs from schools evident in the young people migrating into the cities and selling in the streets and some who are street children. The government used some of the HIPC money to build classrooms but there are still many places, especially in the rural areas, which do not have proper classrooms as the children study under trees. There are many students who do not make it to the tertiary institutions, not because they did not qualify but because of lack of facilities.

ii.   Health: Health care is a major area of concern in Ghana as many of the citizens do not have access to proper health care. This is particularly true of the people in the rural areas, many of whom have no clinics and are far from the major clinics and hospitals.

The incidence of HIV/AIDS, Malaria and other diseases are a problem in Ghana. Though Ghana has initiated programmes like the National Health Insurance Scheme (NHIS) to boost the health needs of the people it has not caught on well with the majority of the population.

iii.   Politics: How many of the citizens are politically active in terms of grassroots decision-making process and also active debate on developmental issues in the communities? Are such decisions left to only the opinion leaders like the chiefs, the assembly representatives or prominent citizens?

The irony of the situation is that, Ghana is a country which is rich in natural resources like gold, diamond, bauxite, timber, and agricultural products like cocoa but her people are poor.

How can this situation be reversed so that Ghana can reach somewhere in her developmental effort? Maximo Torero and Joachim von Braun (2006, p.1) have insinuated that, "ICT diffusion is reaching developing countries, bringing with it high hopes of positive development outcomes." Can this be the case of Ghana? This is the area of concern in our next discussion.

2.4 ICTs and Development of Ghana

As stated in the introduction ICTs are so crucial for development that without it a country cannot make any substantial progress in terms of development. What then is the major reason for development? In the view of Marbub ul Huq (2006), "The basic purpose of development is to enlarge people's choices. In principle, these choices can be infinite and can change over time. People often value achievements that do not show up at all, or not immediately, in income or growth figures: greater access to knowledge, better nutrition and health services, more secure livelihoods, security against crime and physical violence, satisfying leisure hours, political and cultural freedoms and sense of participation in community activities. The objective of development is to create an enabling environment for people to enjoy long, healthy and creative lives." There are proponents that advocate the use of ICT as a factor for development in developing countries.

There are also those who are against the use of ICT for development in developing countries, and the third one being those of the contextualized approach who emphasize on the socio-economic and cultural context of development. Björn-Sören Gigler gives an excellent explanation of the three approaches in this way, "The proponents of ICTs ('World Bank 2002, UNDP 2001) take an optimistic view and highlight the positive effects of the internet and other forms of ICTs to create new economic, social and political opportunities for developing countries and the poor. Its critics on the other hand , take a pessimistic view and claim that ICTs due to existing socio-economic inequalities will favor the privileged segments within society and not reach the economically and socially disadvantaged thus leading to a widening of the socio-economic gap within countries (Panos, 1998, Wade, 2002, Dagron, 2001). Finally, the contextualized approach to ICTs underscores the importance of the socio-economic and cultural context, which is being considered crucial for the better understanding of the potential effects of ICTs on development and the empowerment of poor communities (Avgerou, 2001; Walsham, 1993 and 1998)."

In his critique of the approaches Björn-Sören Gigler (2004) said that in spite of their significant difference, all three approaches share one key feature in common in that the focal point of their investigation represents technology and its societal,

21

economic and political impact. He again observed that these different schools of thought distinguish themselves by emphasizing either the positive or negative impacts of ICTs on people's lives, or stress that the impacts will vary depending on the local and social context in which the ICT program is being carried out.

I go with the view that ICT can be a factor of change in Ghana to bring about development. This will make Ghana bridge in a small or bigger measure the digital divide between her and the developed world. The present government has made ICT one of the major priorities of its policy and it is important to put this in practical terms and provide computers, Internet, cell phones, videoconferencing to poor rural communities in order to enable them to overcome the existing digital and knowledge divide.

It is interesting to note that distance learning on Television is broadcast for students but how many people in the rural areas have access to Television? This is for the advantage of the city dwellers who already have good schools. There should be many mobile vans going to deprived areas to expose them to ICT. Access to ICT can be revolutionary as the people can be opened to a new world of information and create the need to improve their lives. In the words of Björn-Sören Gigler (2004), "The improved access to information and ICT skills can enhance poor people's capabilities to make strategic life choices and to achieve the lifestyle they value."

The people will then make a choice in their lives. They will see the need for electric power in remote areas and that may call for immediate action to provide affordable energy. The exploration of solar energy can be a choice. What is important for me is that the individual person and the community make a choice and that is what is important for development. The need for development should not be imposed but should come from within. It is important for the people to be exposed to the benefits of ICTs and then they can make the strategic choice and their hearts and minds will be in it and work at it with total commitment and passion for their own good and transformation.

As the saying goes "Knowledge is power" and this is what ICTs do for the people. ICTs empower the people through making it easier for them to access wide variety of information for their use. The students gain more knowledge about their environment and the world around them. Farmers are made aware of new techniques in an easier way and can improve their yields. They can also be exposed to the wider markets and this will open their horizon to think of producing not only for internal consumption but also for export. This is not only in the agricultural sector but also other goods and services.

The people can also learn from other cultures and this will help in cross-cultural exchange and understanding. ICTs would also make people appreciate what they have and see how they could incorporate into their system so as to make their lives better.

ICTs would also make people more politically conscious and thus participate in all the levels of political activities in their communities so as to work for the communal good. The people get easy access to information and that bridge the gap between the cities and the rural areas.

There are many government institutions and corporation which do not have access to ICTs and those which have used old typewriters and old computers which are dysfunctional. We now live in a global village where speed and competition count a lot for one to participate fully in the new economy. It is being abreast with ICTs that one can reap the benefit thereof.

2.5 What are the Challenges?

There would certainly be some challenges to face when using ICTs to initiate and accelerate the development of a people. ICTs facilities are expensive and it calls for high capital investment when one wants to chalk some successes. The government is faced with other commitments and it is only when it sees ICTs as the engine to propel the growth and development of the nation that more funds could be channeled through it.

The other challenge is that a large number of the people do not have access to ICTs. As is the case of the many universities in Europe and America where all the students and staff have internet access provided by the universities and assignments and lectures are posted online, this is not the case in the Ghanaian universities. If this is the case in the tertiary institutions then we can see the enormity of the problem.

There is also a high rate of computer illiteracy in the country. Since about 70% of Ghanaians live in the rural areas and many do not have access to electricity and telephone facilities and for that reason cannot use computers let alone connected to the internet, we can conclude that same percentage are computer illiterate and that is a big problem for the nation. Even in the cities connection to the internet is so expensive that the ordinary Ghanaian cannot afford. The internet cafes are also expensive and in a situation when one has to think about what to eat, wear and sleep, the choice is obvious. It is no wonder that, as stated by Opoku Ankomah (2004), Africa in general is described as "the most unconnected in an increasing connected world"

It seems that ICTs in the rural areas would be a mirage. This is because for ICTs to be operational there is the need for a computer, a telephone line, an internet provider and electric power. In the words of Maximo Torero and Joachim von Braun (2006, p.67), ICTs are not like simple consumables like bread but ICTs must be consumed with other products.

Some of the biggest challenges facing developing countries are as the World Bank Report (2006) puts it "weak policy and implementation capacity, opposition from vested interests and persistent obstacles to adoption of ICTs.

2.6 Recommendations

I am aware of the many efforts that the government is making to promote ICTs. This is seen in making ICTs one of its major priorities. We see this policy put into practice by an act of parliament creating the Ghana's National Development Policy (ICTAD) to among other things, facilitate ICTs infrastructural development. There is also the Kofi Annan ICT Centre of Excellence located at Teshie to train people in Ghana and other African countries in ICT to champion ICT development in the African Sub-region. There are many other initiatives by the government of Ghana to promote ICT but these are not far reaching enough to touch the poor and those in the rural areas. It is for this reason that I make the following recommendations.

i. Many young people should be especially trained in ICTs and then empowered to reach out to the rural areas. A set of people from a district can be selected, trained and then given the necessary tools to go to their communities to train others. This will make

ICTs accessible to the less privileged in the society otherwise it will widen the gap between the privileged and the under privileged in the society.

ii. The teaching and exposure to the computer and the internet should start from the primary schools through to the secondary schools. The departments and the whole universities should be equipped with computers and internet so that the students can make use of them for their academic work. It makes studies easier, faster and flexible.

iii. The government alone cannot make ICTs for all possible in the shortest time. This calls for the involvement of the private sector, which the government has identified as the engine of growth, the Religious bodies, chiefs and all interested people should see to the implementation of ICTs in the communities for use by the people, especially the youth, who are the future of the nation. So both formal and informal donor support groups and international bodies through the south-south cooperation should all play a part in making ICTs a factor of change in developing countries and in our case Ghana (Abdul Basit Haggani, 2005, p.44)

iv. It is important for the government to monitor, evaluate and guide investments in ICTs and connectivity in the country, especially in the rural areas.

2.7 Conclusion

We have looked at how ICTs can be a factor of change in a developing country like Ghana. We looked at the various sectors that the use of ICTs can bring about development in Ghana like the educational, economics, social and other areas of the people's lives. But these are not without concomitant challenges. We underlined the main challenges as funds and commitment to change and improvement in one's way of life. We made suggestions as to what can be done to promote ICTs and here we called for other organizations to support the government effort in making ICTs a case for development in Ghana. We are presently in the digital age and no nation can afford to be left behind as this will call for the doom of the nation and so for Ghana, ICTs is not a choice, it is a MUST.

Chapter Three

3.0 The Symbolism of Water in Africa

3.1 Introduction

Water is life. All living things need it to live so it plays a very important and crucial role in our lives. It is for this reason that we have the International Water Day, which grew out of the 1992 United Nations Conference on Environment and Development (UNCED) in 1992 in Rio de Janeiro, to raise awareness of the importance of water and its judicious use in the world. In this essay I would like to look at symbolism of water in Africa drawing special examples from Ghana.

In Africa, due to the warm weather conditions it is important that one drinks a lot of water to make up for the lost fluid in the body. In Europe it was always a surprise when I asked for water to drink in any of the households I visited. But I kept on saying that 'water is life' and for us Africans it plays a very important role in our lives. There have been many efforts made to get clean water for rural communities in Africa through the drilling of boreholes but I must say that the people face many difficulties in the area of potable water delivery. This is even a problem in the towns and cities.

3.2 Water in Africa

When one talks about the problem of water accessibility in Africa, I am sure that people in the Western world find it difficult to imagine and understand this issue in Africa. This is because water availability is unquestionable. Water is in abundance and is properly harnessed and for that matter water is even taken for granted. I have lived in Germany for some years now and have never come across water shortage or the taps not flowing, a situation which may be only a dream in many African countries.

Like many other resources in Africa, Africa as a whole is blessed with major water bodies. We have big and small rivers. Rivers like the Nile and lakes like the Victoria are found in Africa. The rainfall situation is encouraging, except for some few areas like Ethiopia, where there are occasional drought resulting in famine. The desert regions have oasis which are really a blessing to the inhabitants .The desert dwellers have their sources of water from the oasis.

The problems we have had with regard to water in Africa are flooding which result in loss of lives and properties. In my own country, Ghana, whenever we have heavy downpour of rain there is always flooding in certain parts of the country leading to destructions. Interestingly, subsequent governments always make promises to contain and solve the problem but they just have to wait till the following year to make the same promise.

The other serious issue is pollution. Streams and rivers are polluted leading to the presence of certain diseases like guinea worms, river blindness, and Cerebra-Spinal Meningitis (CSM). In such villages and towns, we need to provide them with clean potable water. This is the area where bore holes for water are needed. Through the provision of water in this way the people are able to get good drinking water for their livelihood. That is why it is very heart-warming to have people taking water project as their apostolate, drilling boreholes in the rural areas of Africa. Interestingly, this initiative is taken by Westerners through the generosity of people who have Africa at heart. But it is important that the Africans themselves also take some initiatives to solve their own problems, especially if we appreciate that water is life and good drinking water is a panacea for good health. When the citizens have good health the nation can make progress in their developmental efforts.

In Africa a symbol is the most effective means of communicating our philosophy, theology and life to the world. Africa has rich and reflective symbols which depict, typify and represent their culture. It would therefore be interesting and proper to dilate on the symbolism of water in Africa.

As I discuss this topic I want us to be aware that Africa is a big continent with diverse cultural groupings. There are thousands of them and so it would be difficult to touch on the symbolism of water in all these cultures. So I want to limit myself to Ghana and even here to some of the major cultural groupings. I would also take the elements mostly common to all these cultures.

3.3 Childbirth

Water is the source and sign of life, a sign of God's blessing for his people. In view of this it features prominently in the lives of the people from childbirth to death.

On child birth, there is a belief, among the Akan of Ghana, that a new-born child is coming from another and different world and so it is important to cut off all the connections that the child might have had with the world it came from. The child is therefore washed with water to effect this kind of separation. This is very much related to our

Christian baptism whereby the baptized is bathed or sprinkled with water so as to lead him or her from the world of darkness to the world of light.

During the course of the first bath a drop or two drops of water is made to drain on the child's tongue to welcome it into this world.

3.4 Naming

Child naming is one of the most important aspects of the African culture. Among the Akans of Ghana during naming ceremonies, water and wine are used as symbols of honesty and integrity. The head of the family who officiates at the naming ceremony dips his right forefinger into water and wets the child's lips with the water three times. While doing this he mentions the child's name each time. He does the same with the wine. The child is made to take the two and instructed to differentiate between the two always. The significance of this is that, the child should grow to become truthful and let its 'yes' be 'yes' and 'no' be 'no. He should be able to differentiate between good and evil.

This has a correlation with our Christian baptism. We profess in baptism to be Christ-like in all things, upholding truth and renouncing falsehood also at all times.

Among the Ga of Ghana however, the elder takes a calabash full of water and throws it on the roof three times so that it trickles down onto the child like rain. The purpose is to introduce the child to rain and the earth. Both rain and the earth are seen as gods. The rivers and streams are therefore deified as goddesses, so in this case rain is seen as coming down from the male god of the sky.

3.5 Puberty

Puberty is a stage in the life of the African child whereby he or she has now reached a new stage in life, a life of adulthood. Puberty rites are performed to effect this transition to adulthood. In some cultures in Africa young boys also go through the puberty rites. They are circumcised, they learn how to fight, hunt and are introduced to the use of weapons. They are taught how to fire a gun or use bows and arrows. It is a sign of courage and bravery to have mastery of these weapons. This example can be found among the Ada ethnic group of Ghana.

The girl who has reached the stage of puberty undergoes many rituals. After the rituals the girl is then sent to a stream or river where she is thoroughly bathed to render her clean. Where there is no stream or river water can be put in a basin for the same purpose. On arrival at the stream the officiating woman removes her cloth and dips her into the stream three times and informing the spirits of the water of their presence and purpose. Water here serves as a means of purification and also to introduce the girl to the spirit of the river for protection and guidance.

This above ceremony gives us the idea that in Africa water symbolizes a god and the people consult this god for their needs. The Ogba people of Nigeria have such a belief. They refer to these waters as 'egbamini' (boundary waters). The river gods are consulted before a war or consulted to have more children. The Ogba people believe that the 'Egbamini' cannot do evil.

3.6 Death

The African believes in life after death. So before a person dies, he or she is given water to drink. It is believed that everybody goes to continue his or her life after death and so water, as an essential source of life, must be given to a dying person in order for the person to go and continue his or her life in the ancestral world.

Water is given to the dying to sustain him or her to undertake the long journey to the ancestral world. Some believe also that one crosses a river with a boat to the other world.

Again, every dead body must be washed with water before it is buried so that one can go to the ancestors as a clean person.

During funerals when the people return from the cemetery, water mixed with some herbs is placed at the entrance of the house where the funeral is held.

All those who came from the cemetery are to wash their hands in this water. Some see this as an act of hygienic practice but generally it is regarded as a sign of purification and also for driving out all evil or bad spirit they might have contracted at the cemetery. Even though the people erect monuments at the cemetery to symbolize that their people are not really dead but have attained a new state of life and still live among them, there is also the belief that the cemetery is a place where evil spirits dwell.

3.7 Widowhood

Widows and widowers are made to bath three times a day for a certain number of weeks with water to sever every relationship (physical) he or she might have had with the dead spouse and also to make him or her clean to begin life anew. Among the Kasena Nankana people hot and cold water is thrown at the widow and if in case she gets burned then it indicates that the widow had been unfaithful to her husband. It is important to point out that the penal code in Ghana makes it unlawful the practice is still going on. The Catholic Church is trying to do something about it through her inculturation process but it is one of the die-hard cultural practices in Ghana.

3.8 Real Life Situation

A curse is a dangerous thing in many cultures in Africa, especially south of the Sahara. A curse may lead to hardship and even death. A curse arouses the wrath of the gods and water is needed to cool them down. Water is needed in trying to recant the effects of a curse uttered. An example of such a god is The 'Thunder god' also called 'Sango'.

When there is a quarrel between two people or two factions and the issue has been settled water is used to pour libation to the gods. In the libation the ancestors are asked to take the drink and fight against their enemies, the evil forces, and should drink the water so as to bring them peace and prosperity.

The African sees water as a gift or favor from God. It is a symbol of their being at peace with their object of worship (God). When there is drought, they see it as a sign of divine displeasure with them. So in many cases ritual sacrifices are made to appease the gods and the ancestral spirits. A classic example is what happened in Zimbabwe in 1992, when there was drought and the people sought the help of some spiritualists. The three main groups from which the people sought their advice were the Ngele Reform, Juliana Movement and the Manyangwa Theological Reform.

Among the Trio people of the Congo a woman who wanted an increase in the fertility of the soil could go to a twin who would bless water for her. She would sprinkle this water all over her field to induce fertility for her soil. In addition to this the Trio people use water for divination. This is called hydromancy. The diviner gazes into water and foretells the future.

3.9 Welcome

There are many ways by which Africans welcome strangers, visitors and their relations who have travelled and have come back home. Among the Yoruba and Ibo of Nigeria, they present kola nut as a sign of welcome. In Ghana, in the northern cultures the visitor is given a drink called 'pito' or 'brukutu' made from maize. But in the south water is mainly given to the visitor by the host before greetings are exchanged. The giving of water goes beyond its literal sense of quenching thirst. It indicates the readiness of the host to accept and welcome the visitor. The refusal to give water to a visitor may indicate enmity and can thus be a cause for complaint before elders. Water therefore is a symbol of love, peace, friendship and hospitality.

3.10 Festivals

In many of the festivals we have in Ghana, the symbolism of water features prominently. Among the Gas of Ghana, water is fetched into a basin and some herbs are added to it and prayers said. The 'wulomo' or the fetish priest carries the basin amidst singing and dancing and the basin is carried through the principal streets. It s believed that the sins of the people are collected and thrown into the sea to bring to the people forgiveness and prosperity.

In the 'Asafotufiam' festival of the Ada of Ghana the people bathe in the mighty waters of the Volta to wash clean of their sins and evil and to ask for the gods and ancestors' blessings. Those who have been barren ask for children and others ask for various needs.

In the 'Odwira' festival of the Ashante of Ghana among the various rites is the procession at 2:00am with the blackened ancestral stool to the stream for ceremonial washing in the river.

In scripture the use of water as a source of purification is very prominent. The story of Naman the leper who was healed by the prophet Elisha comes readily to mind. There is also the story of the blind man who could not get anyone to help him into the river and so others got ahead of him and had their healing. The essence of the story is that the people were healed through water, which is stirred by the angels.

In the Church water is used in some of the sacraments, for instance, in baptism and the Holy Eucharist. The water used in baptism washes away the sins of the people. The people are purified and made a new creation.

During the celebration of the Holy Eucharist and blessings of persons, homes and articles water is blessed and sprinkled upon the people as a sign of driving out evil and praying for God's blessing upon the people. In the Holy Eucharist also, water is added to the wine whiles the priest prays that, "By the mystery of this water and wine may we come to share in the divinity of Christ, who humbled himself to share in our humanity".

3.11 Conclusion

The symbolism of water in Africa communicates to us the faith that the African has in water. It occupies a fundamental aspect of their lives as a people. They believe in it, it brings them together in times of division, it nourishes their love for one another, it helps them to live honest and upright life as a people, it makes them aware of the social situation in their communities and it prepares them for a better life in the next world.

Since water is the source of life for Africans, everyone should reflect on how to reach out to people without water so that they can have access to potable water in order that can prevent diseases of every kind and enhance the dignity of the people. When a person's dignity is enhanced ours is also enhanced, when one person dies of disease through drinking infected water part of us also dies.

The onus therefore lies on Africans to make potable water available, sustained and affordable to the people.

Chapter Four

4.0 The Role of the Media in Ghana's Democracy

4.1 Introduction

Democracy is being championed in Africa due to the fact that in many of the countries in Africa, especially in Sub-Saharan Africa, military dictatorship has been the order of the day and that has led to the deepening of poverty and insecurity on the African continent. One of the countries in Africa that has made a significant change from military rule to democracy is Ghana. The acceptance, practice and entrenchment of democracy in Ghana has made her a classic example for the many other African countries. One institution that has played a major role in the development of democracy in Ghana is the media. In this paper therefore, I shall look at democracy, its tenets and practice in Ghana; the problems that have characterized the institutionalization of democracy in Ghana, the new democratic dispensation and the role that the media have played in making democracy functional in Ghana; the successes and challenges and recommendations on making the media more efficient and effective in making democracy workable and sustainable in Ghana.

4.2 Definition of Terms

Two terms which are very important to be defined are *democracy* and *media*. Democracy may mean differently to different people but the one I am going to talk about is the classic definition of Democracy given by Abraham Lincoln as, the government by the people, of the people and for the people. In democracy the people are very much in the centre of politics as they participate in the making of the government by means of election and also being elected into political office. The people are represented in government and so the government is accountable to the people who elected them. That is why democracy is also called participatory democracy. The definition given in the online *Britannica Concise Dictionary* sums it all as, "Form of government in which supreme power is vested in the people and exercised by them directly or indirectly through a system of representation usually involving periodic free elections"

The media on the other hand is from the singular word medium, which means the main means of mass communication. These include Television, the Internet which supports the social media like facebook, tweeter, etc. and E-mail, and even cheap telephony, the Newspapers and Magazines, Telecommunications like the telephones, including the mobile telephony and fax. We can also mention music. The media exist to educate, inform and entertain people. Through the media people get information about the events taking place in the world. I must make mention of the problems that are also associated with this as some people confuse the mediated view of the media with the reality. In the media one communicates information to another to influence the other to a kind of action or inaction. Lasswell stated it succinctly when he writes that, "Who says what to whom in what channel with what effect". Here, Lasswell touches on the whole aspects of the media. These are the communicators, the message, the receivers, the channels and the effects that the media have on people. In this discussion on the role of the media, I will to look at the media in totality in relation to the definition of Lasswell and how this is affecting the democratic process in Ghana.

4.3 Tenets and Practice of Democracy

It is important to look at the tenets and practice of democracy so as to appreciate their importance and the need to work to make democracy viable and operational in Ghana through the use of the media.

In a democratic state the people are able to make decisions that affect their lives, engage in social relationship of their choice and enjoy basic human rights and freedom, like right to life, property, assembly, free speech and religion. Lakoff says democracy is a social and political system characterized by a high degree of personal liberty and equally high degree of political liberty, manifested in regular and free competitive elections, protected by a legal system based upon a constitution, and often articulated by means of federalism (Lakoff, 1996, p.32).

In democracy the individual enjoys personal freedom and thus maximizes his or her opportunities for self-determination. The ability to participate in decision making that affect the individual and living under those decisions is important for the growth and wellbeing of a person. In the words of Larry Diamond the democratic process promotes human development in terms of the growth of personal responsibility and intelligence, while also providing the best means for people to protect and advance their shared interests (Diamond, 1999, p.3). I should say that in democracy we say that the majority carries the vote or the majority is always right. To me this may be a wrong assumption since the majority may be wrong at certain times, likewise the minority may also be wrong at certain times. What can make democracy a good practice is when decisions are made after a high degree of reasoning and objectivity in one's approach to issues and not emotional and personal interest as Plato postulates in his arguments with the Sophists. It is also for human beings to always access what decisions they have made and objectively review for a better approach to move forward in growth and development.

In democracy, there are certain expectations. These are tolerance of the other person's view point; one is expected to be critical in his or her thinking and approach to issues and decision making; one must participate in discussions geared towards the wellbeing of the state or nation; power is vested in the people and not in the hand of one person, so everyone must be empowered in one way or the other so that power does not rest in one person but all through individuals being responsible and getting on board in the politics of the society. This is because all human beings are affected in every aspect of their lives by politics, so no one can stay aloof.

4.4 Democracy in Ghana

Ghana gained her independence from the British on the 6th of March 1957 and became the first Sub-Saharan African country to gain political independence. Since then, Ghana experienced series of military interventions until 1992 when it embraced again constitutional government and this has continued till today. In the *Afrobarometer briefing Newspaper*, which is a paper produced by a group of eminent social scientists from 16 African countries, there is a report in the August 25 edition that, in a poll that was undertaken by the group, it was evidenced in the poll that democracy was still the preferred form of government for 75 percent of Ghanaians and 82 percent reject one party rule or any form of military takeovers.

The burgeoning democracy in Ghana is something to write home about. A former president of Ghana, J.A. Kuffour, is quoted to attest to this fact when he said "Now there is freedom everywhere and people are not afraid to express their views and even insult the president. This is the price we have to pay for democracy, and it is a good price to pay."

Democracy with all its tenets is to an extent in operation in Ghana. The rule of law is functioning, the fundamental human rights of the people are respected and there is the freedom of the press. Now, we want to look at the role that the media is playing in securing and sustaining the democracy in Ghana.

4.5 The Media and Ghana's Democracy

The media is usually described as the fourth estate of the realm. In other words, the media plays a significant role in the society and this must be acknowledged. Richard Gunther and Anthony Mughan have stated that, "The mass communication media are the connective tissue of democracy" (Gunther, C., & Mughan A., 2000, p.1). This statement again underscores the importance of the media to democracy as they impact on the lives of the people. There have been arguments as to the effect of the media on the people, whether the media can change the attitude of the people or reinforce these attitudes. We shall come back to this point.

The Constitution of Ghana guarantees the right of freedom of expression and the press and here the press includes other forms of media like books, newspapers, newsletters, fliers, posters, paintings, graphics, songs, films, town criers and other forms of folk or traditional communication. We can find this in Sub-section 1(a) of Article 21 of the Constitution of Ghana which says that, "All persons shall have the right to freedom of speech and expression, which shall include freedom of the press and other media" and also Article 18 guarantees the citizens the right of private media ownership (Ogbodah, C., 2004).

There have also been changes in some laws which were considered obnoxious to media freedom. This was the abrogation of the 1963 Newspaper Licensing Law. Chris Ogbondah quotes Flanz who stated that, "Article 162(3) of the new Constitution now makes it an offence for anyone to require newspaper licensing as a prerequisite for publication. It provides that, "There shall be no impediments to the establishment of private press or media; and in particular, there shall be no law requiring any person to obtain a license as a prerequisite to the establishment or operation of a newspaper, journal or other media for mass communication or information" (Ogbonah, C., 2004). Article 162(2) guarantees that "there shall be no censorship in Ghana."

It is important to state here that religious bodies are denied private ownership of a radio and television network but they can have their own newspapers and magazines. Since this is not enshrined in the constitution it could be said to be a limitation on the freedom of ownership and expression.

What I want us to look at is the fact that in Ghana there are government owned National Daily Newspapers like the *Daily Graphic* and the *Ghanaian Times*. There is the Private Newspapers which are also vibrant. Many of them are owned by political parties or members of political parties.

Examples are *The Statesman* and *The Palava*. These papers are mostly writing according to their philosophy and political alignment and agenda. The Religious bodies also have their newspapers and one of them is that owned by the Catholic Church called *The Standard*. There are also magazines in circulation but most of them are foreign ones like *The Ovation* and *West Africa* magazines. There is one government Television station called the Ghana Broadcasting Corporation, This is responsible for radio and television broadcast in Ghana, but there are over one hundred and twenty five FM stations in Ghana. There is a proliferation of internet usage but this is mainly in the major cities and it is accessed by students and people of the middle class and above. There are therefore many people who have no access to the internet or have never touched one before since majority of the people live in the rural areas.

The media in Ghana have been very much involved in the elections in Ghana. The government television stations did creditably well in the allocation of time to the various parties. There were little complains and lapses but in general it was accepted as better than previous times.

Richard Gunther and Anthony Mughan assert that universally it is agreed that the media are of paramount importance in shaping the behavioral and attitudinal orientation of citizens. I consent to this to be true with regards to politics as the people sometimes change their loyalty to a party because of the media content. This happens in the elections in Ghana. For instance during the 2000 elections the governing party of the National Democratic Party (NDC) was sure to win but lost the election because the media was really hard on the ruling government. The same thing happened to the New Patriotic Party government which lost the elections in 2008/9.

The interesting thing is that the same thing is not happening when it comes to changing the behavior of the people in terms of certain environmental practices, like keeping the city clean. It is so difficult to see positive results. The campaign against indiscipline, which has been carried out frequently by the media, seems to have fallen on deaf ears. Politics is something different to the people.

The media has to inform the people on matters that concern their lives and how they can improve upon their livelihood through making their government responsible. As Richard Gunther and Anthony Mughan rightly said, "Informed citizenry is the basis of democracy" (Richard Gunther & Mughan Anthony, 2000, p.273). This means that the citizens should have access to information to ensure that they make responsible and informed choices rather than acting out of ignorance or misinformation. Also, information serves as a "checking function" by ensuring that elected representatives uphold their oaths of office and carry out the wishes of those who elected them (Ogbondah, C., 2004). The media keeps the government on its toes. But I think it should not only be the government that is checked this way, the people should also be made responsible by doing their part in working towards the good of the state. In many instances the media holds the government in check and accountable about corruption whereas to me the highest form of corruption is in the grassroots as in many cases one has to pay something to get what he or she wants. So, I will say that sometimes the decadence at the grassroots reflects that at the top hierarchy of government. It is sometimes the people who make the government corrupt since they give in to corruption or do not raise their voice against the malpractices in the society. The decadence in the society therefore deepens. When the people are quiet about a bad situation just as we have in the spiral of silence theory, the bad situation degenerates and worsens each moment until nothing much can be done about it.

In Ghana the media is active and informs the people through news broadcast and newspaper reviews. What is also gaining currency is the phone-in programmes whereby the citizenry participate in discussions on current issues about government policies and issues making the headlines. This gives credence to the right to freedom of opinion and expression without being controlled. Much as I appreciate this freedom, the problem about this practice is when people give opinion on issues that they do not have any idea about, especially technicalities of law and also things of professional nature. In this way objective professional analysis which is important for solving a problem is lacking and instead of reasoning some people give in to emotions and this does not help democracy. It tears people apart and ferment trouble in the society.

The media in Ghana plays the role of a signaler. In many situations they are very much involved in the agenda setting process of the society. They bring out issues to the public so that the people will think about them. In doing this they create the public sphere. We can cite the example of the media raising the issue of coup d'état in the media in order to make the people think about the option for democracy.

The media also forecast some of the things that may happen in the society. The media propagated the eclipse of the sun which took place in February, 2006. This generated the interest of the people and also helped save many people from damaging their eyes by viewing the eclipse directly with their naked eye. In such situations the unity of the people is felt and this is one of the essences of democracy. For in unity is strength.

The media in Ghana play a watchdog role in the society. They check government officials on corruption and keep the government on its toes. The media brought to light a member of parliament who was arrested for carrying cocaine to the United

States and exposed also top officials who were alleged to be involved in cocaine dealings. Also, the media check on sources of loan of the government from financial institution and expose the existence of these financial institutions and whether these loans would benefit the nation.

The other role played by the media in Ghana is what I will call the representative role. In this we see the media carrying the wishes and aspiration of the people because the people do not have such means to do that or do not understand well the socio-political situation in the country. This is especially in a country where illiteracy is high. There is also the question of fearing to be political as one may be put in a certain category which may not favor a person in his or her life.

Another feature of the media in Ghana, like other places, is playing the advocacy role by providing a platform for competing and conflicting viewpoints. In the view of Reed Kramer, who is a co-founder and chief executive officer of *allAfrica.com*, this is a key to democracy. One of the many advocacy roles played by the media are advocacy against domestic violence, child slavery and child abuse, etc.

One of the main benefits of democracy is development. The media can play a major role in the development of the nation when they help foster democracy. To Reed Kramer, the media have a big role to play in development. Reed Kramer pointed out that, it is very important that as countries debate and determine direction and make choices about resources. That the media is there is to help so that peoples' viewpoints may be heard and sponsor debates on these very vital topics and serve as a forum for all opinions. When there is no democracy growth and development of a nation can be stagnated. One may challenge this assertion by making allusion to a communist country like China which is making a lot of inroads in development. It should be noted that China may be an isolated case but it is important that people develop their own ways of keeping their society together in democracy and foster their own development and expression of their human dignity.

4.6 Successes and Challenges

The media in Ghana have chalked a lot of successes. One of the major successes is fighting for the institutionalization of democracy during the military rule from 1981 to 1992. As stated earlier the media also championed the cause of the people to have new government and this happened when there was a peaceful transition from one democratically elected government to another in the year 2000. The media continues to fulfill its numerous functions and most especially offering a voice to the voiceless as the people also take part in discussing major issues affecting their lives and the entire Ghanaian society. It is also successful in exposing corruption and

56

malpractices in the society and also conscientising the people to abhor military adventurism and work towards the entrenchment of democracy.

The challenges of the media in Ghana today in my view are that most all the journalists publicly have declared their stance or affiliation in terms of political parties. This is not wrong but the problem is that it has affected their objectivity as many of the discussions are done on partisan lines, and so the people who listen to them already form their opinions on these journalists and media networks as to their orientation, and I feel that this does not go well with democracy. Democracy to me is not just having the freedom to express oneself but the freedom to reason and be objective in one's approach to issues for the good of the people and the society. Another challenge of the media now in Ghana is that some of the communicators have assumed the wrong assumption to be masters on every issue and topic. Even though communication studies make one broadminded one does not become expect in everything. So it is important for communicators to know their limitations.

There is also the challenge to better and improve media contents and this involves more training for the personnel and money to access new equipment, especially in the area of Radio, Television, research and outreach. It should also be possible to give some support to newspaper producers so that they can better their quality and content.

The other challenge is the quest to be the first in the news and for which reason sometimes sources are not cross-checked and information are not substantiated with facts before coming on air or publishing things about people. These ways of doing things have marred the reputation of some people in the society since it is not easy to retract information that goes into the public domain, and more so people make up their minds about the issue and not all will read or hear about the retraction. The other effects of this are the many court cases, some of which have led to certain newspapers paying huge sums of money for damages. A case in point is that of Hackman Owusu-Agyeman, the Minister for Works and Housing and a Member of Parliament (MP) for New Juaben who was awarded damages to the tune of 1.5 billion cedis against The Palava newspaper by an Accra Fast Track High Court for defamation of character.

4.7 Recommendations

I have underscored the important role of the media in democracy and looked at the role that the media is playing in the democratic practice of Ghana. In my discussion I tried to give some points for consideration and I wish to reiterate some of the points here and also give some recommendations that can boost the role of the media in Ghana.

The first thing I want us to consider is that some of the media communicators should specialize in certain fields so that they can communicate better and authoritatively in these areas. These areas can be politics, law, social, religion, finance and many others.

In most situations the media is controlled by the government, a political party or some people with some private interest. For the media to play a significant role in democracy there is the need for some degree of autonomy to enable diverse opinions to be discussed dispassionately for the development and good of the nation.

It should be the avowed aim of the media to serve the interest of the people and not their own interest, especially in these days and time when the media has become a money making enterprise with the backing of people with certain agenda and interest. This leads to many advertisements and championing of programmes that bring in money than programmes that educate the people.

Since the internet is gaining grounds in Ghana as one of the means of information dissemination, efforts should be made to make it affordable so that many people can access the internet in their homes, offices and schools. It is interesting to note that in Europe and America which are considered as rich nations, internet access and telephony are becoming cheaper and cheaper whereas in Ghana which is a poor country the cost is so high and only a certain class of people can afford them. It is my view that the regulators step in to check this kind of market practices. The use of the internet should be the commonest thing in Ghana. The internet is servicing as a good medium for political information and debate in the whole world and Ghana cannot be left behind.

The government should continue to uphold the freedom of the press and speech and give all the support that the media needs, especially access to information, so that democracy will continue to be a success story in Ghana.

The media practitioners should also continue to uphold their ethical practices and not be corrupted by officials of government and others with money or favors in order to work effectively and honestly for the good of the society.

4.8 Conclusion

In conclusion, I will say that I have been able to look at democracy and the role that the media is playing in sustaining democracy in Ghana. Some of the problems and challenges that the media encounter as they serve the public through the various networks have been touched on. I offered some recommendations to better the situation of the media in Ghana so as to offer a better service in making Ghana's democracy much more vibrant and an example to the other African nations. The media should teach the people that democracy should not give the opportunity to politicians to subject the people to continuous cycle of poverty whiles the leaders live in opulence. Democracy should lead to teaching the people how to love to see their country and her people developed and progressed by fighting against favoritism, self-centrededness and all kinds of negative behaviors and attitudes.

Chapter Five

5.0 The Making of a New Ghana

5.1 Introduction

When the first president of Ghana DR. Kwame Nkrumah) made the declaration that "Ghana, our beloved country is free forever!" it was surely a new beginning for Ghana. It was a new beginning that gave dignity to the Ghanaian, a new beginning that gave hope of a better and prosperous nation, devoid of poverty, conflicts, diseases and disunity. The question now is what has been the situation of the Ghanaian since then? What can be done to remedy our problems and project Ghana as truly the "Black Star of Africa? These are the issues that we want to discuss in this article.

5.2 Current Situation

Ghana has gone through difficult situations and there have been attempts and efforts by various leaders to fix our problems but our development is not getting faster as it should. Today, a lot of our country folks are wallowing in abject poverty and destitution. We seem divided today more than united on the day of independence. The euphoria that greeted our independence has waned or dimmed. Much as in general there is relative peace in Ghana the theater of inter and intra ethnic conflicts in some of our regions, leading to loss of innocent lives and destruction of property should not be tolerated. On the ethnic issue also, in spite of the improved situations of inter-marriages, many are those, who, because of their own political self interest, have taken advantage of the multi-ethnic nature of our country and are playing on the ethnic cord to divide the people. This is reinventing the colonial tactics of divide and rule. Some governments and their functionaries in Africa talk much about economic indicators showing significant theoretical improvement but the concrete living situation of the majority of the people show otherwise. For Africa to progress this kind of politicking should stop so that they can address the reality, the concrete living situation of the people.

Our environment is not something good to write home about. Most of our surroundings are filthy and even the attempts to make our cities clean are resisted and that makes the efforts of those in charge meaningless. These good intentioned people do not only lose courage in the face of resistance to the change they want to bring about, but are characterized as enemies of the people. Our gutters are filled and choked with debris and our rivers polluted. Trees on river banks are cut down and bushes are burnt, leading to serious environmental consequences. Many people do not have regard for the environment, so we surely have to correct our attitudes on this matter. It is no wonder that we have not been able to fight against malaria and other diseases in our country. Also, no wonder we continue to suffer lack of power because the Volta River is dry.

The influx of young people to the major cities of Accra, Kumasi, Sekondi-Takoradi and other places in Ghana, and lack of employment of many of our young people, have brought about increase in anti-social activities. It is sad to read about daylight prostitution in some parts of our country. This is in the era of HIV/AIDS pandemic. It is even scarier the reports of contract killings and armed-robbery taking place in our country, despite all the security efforts being made to curb the situation. The question is what is happening to our values, what is happening to our country? There is certainly the need to double our efforts to check these anti-social acts among Ghanaians, and foreigners who are taking the hospitality, the calm and peaceful environmental situation in Ghana as our weakness to perpetuate their criminal activities in Ghana.

5.3 Charting a new Path

We cannot conclude the litany of the problems we are facing in our country. It is for this reason that we need to chart a new course, a new programme and effect a concrete and workable change in Ghana and offer positive hope to Ghanaians. We want a new Ghana as envisioned by our founding fathers: a boisterous economy; a people not only seeking and working to live in unity but a people united as one people tied together by a common destiny; a people respecting law and order and upholding justice, fairness and respecting the rights of the individual no matter how low or high, how poor or rich; and also respecting the equality of the genders and making everyone feel secured and protected.

One may ask if we can do what we have stated above, if we can improve on the holistic life of the Ghanaian since much effort have been made by some past leaders, and we are either making marginal progress or the situation gets much more difficult each time and day. This is not something that cannot be done as some may say they look idealistic. In reality, this should be our aspiration and we need to work hard towards achieving them.

What makes our situation unacceptable is the catalogue of the resources we have in Ghana (gold, manganese, bauxite, diamond, salt, timber, etc) and to say that we are poor or that majority of the people live in abject poverty is a big disgrace. When we look at the resources and capacity of Ghanaians, it is a shame to live without regular supply of electricity for almost a year. This is in a situation whereby not even all households have access to electricity. It is a breach on our dignity not to have regular supply of potable water to every household, have our environment littered around and gutters chocked and breading mosquitoes which result in malaria. In most cases we do practically not much to address the situation and only talk about it all the time, and interested mainly in the statistics of malaria cases in a period. May be that will bring in more donor inflow to line the pockets of some people. We should not countenance that many of our people live in abject poverty in a country where every land is fertile and can grow virtually anything that can be sowed on a land. When one goes to Israel and see the kind of land they have and how the people are able to cultivate crops to feed themselves, then we would say that they offer a big challenge to us in Ghana as to how useful we can put our arable land to use for increased in productivity. Again, it is easier in Ghana to breed any animal and poultry as it

67

is demonstrated by small scale farmers. There should not be hunger in a land where there can be plenty of food at a season and all that is needed is to invest heavily in agriculture and also embrace the industrial technology as to how to process and make our products lasting for use by the people and also for export. Small Scale farmers should be supported to expand their enterprise as their success will entice many others, especially the young people, to go into the formal sector of agriculture.

We need to do something urgently to make Ghana a new GHANA. Anytime we go into elections many political parties and their politicians come with their manifestoes and convince the people that they can fix the problems of the nation. This is good since in every nation we need leaders who play a significant role in transforming the destiny of the people, just as Dr. Kwame Nkrumah and others led us into independence. We cannot therefore downplay the leadership factor. But we need a leader who will translate the wealth of the nation into making the life of the people better. The people will have food security and that means aggressive agricultural programme should be implemented. As mentioned earlier, we would like to see concrete plans as to how the person is going to revamp agriculture and improve our storage facilities and build factories to add value to our agricultural products. We would also like to see how the person is going to harness our water resources so that the citizens can enjoy portable water throughout the country: cities, towns and villages. We may not need the process of desalination to provide water to our people but effective management and use of our river bodies for use by the people. This embraces also the generation of power which is essential for the development of the people. Where there is power there is life and progress or development. So, we would like to see a leader who is going to go beyond the traditional power generation in Ghana and embrace solar and wind and even go beyond them. We do not necessary have to follow what is being done elsewhere. We have our scientists and they should be put to work to make certain breakthroughs in the scientific field in Ghana. We would like to see a leader who would challenge and empower our scientists to come out with new innovations relevant to the Ghanaian and African situation. It is not only scientists who should be supported but all the fields of study should be supported to contribute concretely and realistically to the progress of Ghana. One particularly area is architecture, which should feature prominently in the building and construction industry. We have serious housing problem in Ghana as there are many people who do not only have affordable housing but many are those who live in indecent places or are without a place to call home and therefore sleep on the streets. How can we provide low cost but durable housing for our people?

We surely have myriads of problems and these are affronts to our dignity as a people and a nation. What is needed right now is how to build up the people for change and progress.

5.4 How to effect the Change: Some Suggestions

1. Ghanaians have to change their mentality and reorient their attitudes. One particularly area is the attitude that, it is the central government's responsibility to provide them all their amenities, that the central government is responsible for their problems. Much as the central government has a responsibility to the people, it is high time now for the people to take their destiny into their own hand. The people are the government and they should make the people they put in power, who also form the central government responsible. One way of doing this is to look at their environment and access what they need to improve their lot and work and work hand in hand with the government towards its realization. An example is that a district or an area can solve its electrical problem by accessing the situation and sourcing for fund to implement for example solar energy. This fund may

come from the people, government and International Organizations. The same can be in the area of water, road, clinic or hospital and facilities for the youth of the area.

2. Effort of national integration should be undertaken to unite the people much more than we have today. The natural effort of inter-marriages is not enough. There should be concrete plans to achieve national integration for nation building. Nkrumah did this by instituting boarding school where young people of diverse ethnic backgrounds came together to study and thus charted a common path for their country. We would like to see a leader who has a programme of national integration. This may counteract politicians who usually like to play one ethnic group against the other. An example may be learning of additional Ghanaian language, since that helps one to enter into and appreciate the culture of a people. The ideal is to have apart from English as our common language, one unifying Ghanaian language.

3. There should be something which will be a unifying factor for Ghanaians so that we will think and work together as one people with a common destiny. We can open discussion on this issue and it is my conviction that something positive and good would be

arrived at. This is also where our academicians should come out with certain positive ideologies which will make Ghanaians to change their attitudes presently so as to rekindle their spirit of tenacity, hardwork, courage and love for unity and peace.

4. We have many health issues in Ghana and many Ghanaians die of illnesses that would not otherwise have sent them earlier to their graves. This may be that they could not go to the hospital because they did not have money. It is for this reason that the National Health Insurance Scheme (NHIS) is so important and should not be politicized at all. What we need to do is to discuss how to make it better and workable so that the poor people can also live longer and enjoy some life. Our health personnel should also be taken very good care of and supported so that they will stay in Ghana to provide the needed health care. Whenever the health personnel go on strike we lose a lot of patients. We need a government that will not let this happen.

5. Education is so important and the efforts being made in this field is laudable. But no matter these efforts being made in the area of Free Compulsory Basic Education, Feeding Programme, etc., the best way to improve

education is to improve the lot of teachers. When teachers are taken good care of we should be assured that the education policy of the government will work. So much more attention should be given to our teachers in terms of a raise in their salaries, further education, good housing, car allowance and whatever will make them happy. The future of our young people would surely be bright since these teachers would be committed since we would have every right to demand good work from them.

6. The government should find a way of investing in the people of the nation. Everyone should be brought on board in the development agenda. Each and every Ghanaian should be seen as important and whatever it takes to help him or her to achieve his or her fullest potential should be done. It may not be easy but am looking forward to elaborate plan that takes into consideration making every worker more efficient, hardworking, productive and also well-paid. A plan to check unnecessary bureaucracy leading to bribery and corruption at work places. Also, a plan to broaden the tax net and enforce tax laws so that we can generate much more revenue for the development of Ghana. Also,

transparency as to what the taxes of the people are being used for.

7. Sometimes we feel ashamed to see the dilapidated houses of our police force and also the Army. Most of the houses were not build for the large families that some of the service personnel have today. There seem to be improvement but much more work needed to be done in this area. The other motivation of basic amenities and tools needed for their work should be provided on a regular basis. When people are content with themselves and their work, then they can inject much more energy and efficiency into their work. If we needed to chase away the armed robbers, to protect our country and our constitution; we cannot afford to make the lives of these noble men and women a happy one. It is then that we can hold them much more responsible to in keeping law and order in our country. It must also be said that the service personnel should keep their environment clean and beautiful, for example, planting of trees and flowers. This is not something that should be put on the government. They should also be responsible in maintaining the equipment given to them to enhance their work.

5.5 Conclusion

The future is bright for Ghana but one can experience this brightness if we journey together and enter into it together. We hear news of the discovery of oil in greater quantities both offshore and inland. This is making everyone happy. But it should not be like the other resources that we are proud of but their income seems not to reflect on our lives as a people. We need to take our destiny into our own hands. If the multinationals are coming for our oil and we are not going to gain anything to help us out of our poverty then we keep it for the next generation who may have the know-how to get the oil. It is important that every Ghanaian becomes wide awake, responsible and also hold those entrusted with power on our behalf responsible so that they do not take us for granted. In the light of this, much more education should be given to the people about their rights. The National Council for Civic Education (NCCE), which is the agent for such civic education, should modify their approaches and intensify their outreach programmes in educating the people on their inalienable freedom and rights.

We have acknowledged our problems and the fact that we are losing most of our values. We have a lot of potential in both human and natural resources and so there is no excuse for us to wallow in our dismal situation. I have given some suggestions as to some of the things we can do to come out of our problems. I stressed on leadership and our own capacity as a people to make a change. We, as a people, should also know that we have a responsibility to ourselves, our families and our nation. We should be proud of our nationality and together let us build our nation. The present generation needs to sacrifice today by hardwork and perseverance and those yet to come will be ever grateful and proud of us.

Chapter Six

6.0 Involving tomorrow's Leaders in today's leadership

6.1 Introduction

There is no doubt that the adult population are aware of the need to sensitize the youth to come to the realization that they are the future leaders and as such have to prepare themselves adequately to take up leadership roles in all aspects of life. This calls for a lot of work on both sides of the adult population and the youth themselves.

6.2 Characteristics of the Youth

It is obvious from the theme that "tomorrow's leaders" are the youth of today. The youth have fascinating characteristics and these have to be identified, nurtured, enhanced and sharpened so as to be well cultivated and used for their future benefit. The youth are exuberant, energetic, visionaries and dreamers. These characteristics offer hope for a better future for the youth since they can utilize them for their own benefits and that of the society in which they live.

The Catholic Church in her document on *Lay People* from **Vatican II document** says that, "young people enter too rapidly a new social and economic environment. While their social and even political importance is on the increase day by day, they seem unequal to the weight of these responsibilities." (AA No.12). It is in the light of this that the Church asks adults to be anxious to enter into friendly dialogue with the young, where despite the age difference they could get to know and share with one another their own personal riches.

6.3 Youth and Leadership role in the Society

We are looking at how the youth can play active role in today's leadership. We know from the recent census that the youth form a greater percentage of the Ghanaian population. They are eventually going to take over the leadership roles of the adults since nature has made it that the adults will certainly become old, weak and die away. For us to ensure that we have good successors, the adults are to train the young ones to eventually take over from them. This training can be done in so many ways.

There is the need for what I would term "Psychological orientation of the youth." We can also describe it as orientation of the attitude of our youth. The mindset of some of the youth is that it is only adults who are capable and fit for all leadership positions. Some of the adults also think the same way, that, young people cannot take up leadership roles since that is reserved only for adults. The youth should have positive thinking that they are capable of taking any leadership roles. This can be achieved when there is friendly interaction between the youth and adults. The youth should be helped to unveil their potentials and capabilities and their confidence should also be boosted.

We should also work in nurturing responsibility in the youth. There is the conception that the youth are not responsible and for that reason they cannot be trusted with certain leadership positions. We see this in all aspects of life, ecclesiastical and civil. The society is always looking for people who are adults and have experience. We forget that the youth are young and flexible. They can be fashioned in any way that the society thinks fit and proper. This can be done through assigning them roles both in the Church, work place and at home. The problem that the adults have about entrusting certain responsibilities to the youth is that young people make a lot of mistake. What we need to know is that, as the saying goes, "The only real mistake is the one from which we learn nothing." The only way to make the youth responsible is to entrust them with responsibilities and offer them the appropriate guidance and support.

The youth are full of ideas and it is important to welcome their innovative ideas and direct them to achieve their purpose. We live in a culture which in many instances relegates the ideas of young people to the background. That should not be the case at all. There is a saying that "The child who knows how to wash its hand eats with adults." What the youth need to do is to adopt certain skills in presenting themselves and their ideas.

We need to challenge and support the youth to improve on their academic performance and self-image and assist them in their goal setting. This is in view of the fact that knowledge is power and that is one of the means to help young people to study and know their environment and how they can contribute to bring development to their society.

The related issue to the above point is that we should develop a programme to teach the youth to master the spoken word. Their medium of communication should be sound and effective. A good leader should be able to articulate his or her views in a clear, logical and convincing way. As a leader people should like to listen to you and not only that, but obey you. This can happen if the leader demonstrates through his or her communication and interaction with the people respect and humility to other people.

A good leader is one who listens, observes and acts. He also has a positive self-image. He is critical and thinks positively. These attitudes should be inculcated into young people. They are marks of leadership.

There is the need to delegate functions to young people so that they feel involved in the affairs of the society and the Church.

In many situations leadership is in the hands of adults and they use every means to remain at their positions even though not much progress is chalked under their leadership and the future does not also look brighter under them. They sometimes have lost touch with contemporary issues and trends and so their policies and ideas stagnate the growth of the society.

Who are determining the way the society should go today? We have the youth who are engaged in music and that is a powerful means of communication and transformation of the society. Are these youth in music playing positive role models or not for their fellow young people?

It is so great and encouraging to know that some young people are making a breakthrough in technology as some are inventing and coming out with new ideas and inventions.

6.4 Recommendations

The youth need to be given the necessary support and attention so that the new breed of young people will be the architects of a changed Ghanaian and African society in the areas of science and technology.

In helping the youth to acquire leadership skills we should eschew favoritism.

We should not focus our attention only in the young people coming from rich and powerful families. God also chooses the weak and makes them strong.

People who have done many inventions in the world came from poor parentage.

There is also the need for feedback and affirmation of the youth. There is a saying that the one who cuts the trail does not know that it is crooked behind him or her. Feedback will help the youth to improve upon themselves. Recognition, acceptance and affirmation will also boost the morale of the youth in working harder to achieve something better and concrete for the future.

Again, the youth should be helped to offer selfless service. They should be educated on the need to give back to the community. This calls for initiative and also one's preparedness to work sacrificially. It is also important that the society or the parish should develop a pool of trained youth who will train other youth in basic leadership.

This should be a regular feature on the parish/ youth programme.

The concluding point is that it is said that the fear of God is the beginning of wisdom. The fear of God therefore should be inculcated into the youth so that they live good upright and moral lives, especially in these days of promiscuity and disregard to truth, justice and righteousness.

6.5 Conclusion

I have tried to share with you some thoughts on how to involve today's youth in tomorrow's leadership. We need to structurize our youth programmes in Ghana in particular and in Africa as whole, especially at the local levels and in the religious groups. They should emphasize on leadership formation. That is the hope for the society tomorrow in terms of the provision of quality leaders for the society. The youth should be reminded that what they will be in the future depends on what they put in today. The adults on the other hand should know that it is defeatist and a shame not to train leaders to succeed them tomorrow.

Chapter Seven

7.0 Towards an Effective Leadership in Africa: the way forward

7.1 Introduction

The problems that face Africa today are numerous and enormous, and they become worse with each passing day. These problems have been blamed squarely on the absence of good leadership. In a nation where there is lack of good leadership many structures collapse and the nation loses its fine tuning for development and progress. This underscores the fact that good leadership can propel a nation to rapid growth, and the lack of it can stagnate a nation. In this essay therefore, I would like to look at the meaning of leadership, types of leadership, characteristics of leaders, what makes for good leadership, the situation in Africa with regard to leadership and what can be done to make leaders accountable so that they work for the

85

good of their people, their nations and Africa as a whole.

7.2 Leadership

When one carefully examines nature, the obvious thing to see especially among insects and animals is that there are leaders among their various groupings which lead the others so that they can fulfill their needs or reach their aim. Examples could be found among ants, termites, bees, birds, whales and elephants. The Bible tells us that, "Go to the *ant*, O sluggard, and consider her *ways*, and *learn* wisdom" (Proverb 6:6). This is to teach us about leadership and how a good organizational leadership can help a society solve many of its problems. In the human society too, there is the need of a person in any group of people who takes the role of leadership, to effectively influence others so that they can work together as a team in order to achieve their set aim and objective. The word leadership can be well clarified and understood when we look at its meaning from the Latin perspective. It comes from the Latin word, "gubernatio", which apart from standing for leadership gives the idea of directing, commanding, steering and piloting. These words connote action and this shows that there is always the need for someone to be at the forefront or hem of a team to steer things to a successful end, without which the team cannot only achieve their goals but there would be chaos and disaster among the team members. Leadership, therefore simply defined, is the process of someone leading others to attain a common goal.

86

Mike Woodcock and Dave Francis define leadership as the capacity to harness human and other resources to achieve results. This means that the right people should be found to do the right job and the selection should not based on ethnic, political, social or religious considerations. These people who are chosen for leadership should be creative and be able to work with others in the team. They should be focused if they want to achieve their goals for their nation. The leaders therefore must know what they want to do, with what kind of people and with what material and duration needed for the job to be done. With the right people, given the right motivation and perseverance they can be focused to achieve their results.

When we talk of leadership, our minds readily go to political leadership of politicians and traditional leadership of our chiefs and elders in the traditional societies, since in many ways they affect our lives. But there is the broad spectrum of leadership in our society and this could be religious leadership, community leadership and leadership found in the educational institutions, work places, organizations and clubs. Leadership features from the bottom of the society to the topmost level. It is very important to begin training people from the lowest base of the society so that when they gradually rise to the highest level they could understand better the people and situations and offer enhanced and quality leadership.

7.3 Types of Leadership in Africa

Africa has experienced various types of leadership on the political sphere. Some of these leaders have in the course of their rule exhibited more than one type of leadership. There have been autocratic leaders in Africa, where leaders think that they are the repository of knowledge and wisdom and for this reason they do not tolerate criticism from anybody and they kill or incarcerate people with opposing views. Such people manipulate elections and hold on to power even when the people are dying and suffering all because their policies are not working to better the living standard of the people. Many people have suffered under this type of leadership style in Africa. The members of the opposing political parties are usually the targets. They are imprisoned, tortured, killed or they had to run into exile because of persecution from a dictatorial leadership. Unfortunately many of these dictators believe that they have the best policies to free the people and so they needed to use such a strong hand to fight opposition to their vision. As the Akan of Ghana say, "tikoro nko agyina" meaning, "one head does not take counsel". The involvement of people with opposing views help to shape ideas for the betterment of the people.

However, some of the leaders in Africa have been true democrats. They come to power through the process of the ballot box which defines the will of the people. Such leaders believe in the institutions of the state and allow these institutions to operate without undue interference. They also uphold good governance. The people take active part in their own governance and their views are taken into consideration in any policy initiative. The rule of law is upheld and promoted to ensure that everyone obeys the laws of the land, and the state deals equally with people who go against these laws. In a state where the rule of law is in operation, fear of reprisal is discouraged to the highest level and this makes the system operational and trustful. The fruits that such a situation brings to the people are creativity, innovation, motivation, stability, unity and progress. Freedom, justice and peace, which are the cornerstone of any nation, flourish in a better way and this puts the nation in stability and progress.

Much as democracy is a desired form of governance in Africa, there is the need for the leaders to be strong to address the many recalcitrant issues facing countries on the continent. We need to Africanize our democracy. In order words, our democracy should responds to the character, attitude and needs of the people. That is why in my book, The Rescue, I opted for a blend of autocracy and democracy. In this book, I suggested that, the leader should have a mixture of 15% autocracy and 85% democracy, but these percentages may change depending on the situation, the problems and the people, but never should autocracy be the dominant factor. A leader should be able to adjust and adopt leadership style according to the needs of the people at different times.

The above types of leadership are the most obvious ones on the continent. There are other types of leadership like the *laisser-faire* or delegative form of leadership. This is a style of leadership where the leader offers no or little guidance and leaves decision making in the hands of a group. This is only a good style when the members of the group are highly qualified in their areas of specialty, otherwise, there is a problem when members of the team cannot work together due to age differences, different backgrounds, lack of team spirit, or when the members lack the requisite expertise.

In sum, some people are nominated, elected or appointed into office, while others assume office by popular acclamation because of their charisma. Charismatic leadership emerges when there is a national crisis and the people have trust and confidence in someone who has certain appealing qualities to leading the nation to address this problem. Many of such leaders perform creditably well because they have a strong backing of the people.

7.4 Characteristics of Leadership (What makes for good leadership?)

As a young boy growing up and experiencing barracks life at Teshie-Camp, I witnessed and admired the organization of the soldiers and even their families, and this was due to good leadership. Every now and then there were inspections of the barracks so as to keep the barracks clean. It calls for good leadership organization to do this clean up in the barrack. They had at that time women officers who supervised these inspections. One cannot but to grow up with such leadership attitude injected into him or her.

The soldiers were well-organized, disciplined and obedient to their leaders and I could also see the respect of the leaders for their subordinates even if it was a core content of their training and life. The discipline in the army which I witnessed as a child has had a lasting impression on my life and must say that it is for leadership to instill such a discipline since everyone has the tendency to do what he or she likes without recourse to laid down procedures. But such a discipline is not only demanded from the subordinates but more so from the top so that the leadership become a model to the led. The leader should exude some high degree or sense of respect, confidence and trust in himself and also the subordinates. The leader must always know that even though he or she works together with a team, the leader is responsible for setting the direction where he or she and the other members of the team should take. The leader is responsible for where they are going, why they should take a particular direction, how they are to proceed, the things they need for such a mission and encouraging the members when things become difficult and tough. It is like a protagonist role played by film stars in movies. They have to lead well till the end of a film to make viewers happy and satisfied. The leader should be committed to making sure that everything works to distinction. Excellence therefore is the key word.

A leader therefore should have a good vision which he or she wants the other team members to pursue. This vision could be an economic vision leading to success and wellbeing of the people; it could also be political vision aimed at peace and tranquility; religious vision resulting in peaceful living together of the various religious groups; and organizational and group or team vision leading to success in all these areas in the nation. The leader does not only inspire the members of the team but also empowers them to achieve this vision.

Many are those who in their lives sometimes have fear to face new ideas and technological developments, like the computer and internet. Their immediate reaction to this new form of advancement is to resist because it is too much for them. It is up to the leader to create and inspire confidence in these people so that they also join the bandwagon to bring out something new and unique in themselves and in the society.

The leader is expected to be frank and genuine to the people that he or she leads. Even though the leader may have certain sterling qualities the awareness that he or she is not a super human being but as human as any member of the team is important. The leader is quick to recognize his or her faults and short-comings and tries to overcome them so that he or she can offer better leadership. For this reason leaders are advised to constantly upgrade and develop themselves to better their skills so that they can better lead the people in every situation.

Furthermore, a leader should know that challenges may come his or her ways and sometimes they are surely daunting challenges but it is up to the leader to weather these challenges and this is only possible if the leader has confidence in himself or herself and also enjoys the support of the people. The leader and the people do not give up until they have overcome these challenges or hindrances.

In a nutshell, there are people who are born leaders but there are also people who learn the art of leadership. In either case a leader strives to build up good and enduring relations with other people and he or she is ever ready to serve them even to the point of laying down his or her life for the people. A good leader is happy that he or she leaves something worthwhile for the next generation and when he or she is no more the leader is happy that someone can take over from there and continue the good work.

The above characteristics go for good leadership. There are people who assume leadership role with the sole intention of making their lives and that of their families comfortable, thus stressing up the people they lead and it is not their concern if the people would suffer and die. They think only of themselves. Such people are not leaders but usurpers, self-centered people and do not fit to be called leaders. This is the situation that Africa finds itself today and hence its underdevelopment.

One characteristic of leadership which Africans like very much is a charismatic person. A person who is an orator, eats, work, sing, dance, laugh and weeps with them. Such a charismatic leader is loved and supported by the people. It is therefore important that such charisma be properly used to unite the people for a common purpose. Unfortunately, the lives of most political charismatic leaders are cut short through military take-overs. What the people need here is a person who is a good communicator and can bring out clearly his or her ideas for the people to execute for progress. It is an added advantage if leadership flows naturally from such a person. The leadership Africa needs today is someone who can bring people of all the political parties for a common purpose. He or she recognizes that the problems in the nation is so huge and cannot do it alone by one party but needs the support of all the other parties and people who are non-partisan to effect any meaning change in the nation.

The leaders are expected to exhibit some core values in their lives, such as integrity, honesty, probity and accountability and the fear of God. These values guide the leader in his or her dealing with the people and affect also the governance style of the leader.

7.5 Leadership in Africa

Before the advent of colonialism and democracy, most African people practiced the monarchical system of governance. In this way power rested in the hands of a few royal families and the rule of a people was through kings or queens. These kings and queens have shaped the history of the African people since time immemorial. It is therefore important to note that in this day of democracy chieftaincy institutions have stood the test of time and they are still functional and influential in today's socio-political environment. The chiefs and queens have still significant role to play in shaping the destiny of Africa since they are closer to their people at the grassroot level and can be the engine of transformation in the African societies. They have not outlived their usefulness at all. The question is how to get them effectively aboard in a democratic dispensation so that their leadership would unite the people for productivity and not for violence due to chieftaincy litigation and fighting among the royal family members as to who occupies the stool or who should be enskined? The current state of enlightenment which has brought in literacy and technological way of historical recording should put

94

in place the rightful ways of inheritance so that the process is not manipulated by people who think they can win the seat through their money, governmental or societal influence. These are the core problems of chieftaincy litigation and sustained violence in many African countries. Where there is this sort of violence one cannot think of any improvement in the lives of the people.

Politicians, as we know them today, emerged on the African scene when they had to agitate to fight against colonialism in the quest to claim back their freedom and lands for Africa. Many of them suffered and others died in the course of fighting for freedom. This eventually led to democracy in Africa, but many of the first leaders of Africa instead of transforming the lives of their people sought rather to satisfy their own quest and happiness and thus fought against democracy and perpetuated themselves in power. But this was not the way that democracy operates. One comes to power and following democratic principles enshrined in the constitution can be voted into power again in a free and fair elections. When the people judge the person and the party as doing a good work, then they can vote them back into power. This was the case with exemplary leaders like Olusegun Obasanjo of Nigeria and Flt. Lt. Jerry Rawlings and John Agyekum Kuffour of Ghana. They did not hang on to power when their constitutional mandate was over but handed over peacefully to their successors. But to change the constitution to rule perpetually was a clear indication that such leaders have their own personal agenda. This kind of attitude prompted military take-overs in many

African countries. The irony of the matter is that the military people too began to love power and so entrenched themselves in power for their own interest. Such problems in Africa have continued until now. A case in point is the Presidential Elections in the Republic of Côte d'Ivoire. It is impossible to imagine that this is happening in the 21st Century. The Electoral Commission announced that the Opposition Candidate, Alassane Ouattara has won the elections, but the Constitutional Council overturned the results in favor of the incumbent president Laurent Gbagbo for a third term. This is not something new in Africa. It has happened in recent times in Kenya, Zimbabwe and now in the Republic of Côte d'Ivoire. Many African leaders and their parties find it difficult to cede power to their opponents. Such constant inter-party strives contribute to underdevelopment in Africa. Much fruitful time is used to undermine the other party in or outside governance and the country continues to suffer. This is why the former United Nations Secretary -General slammed the "Pull Him Down" (PHD) syndrome or attitude in African politics and deplored the undoing of the work of their predecessors for political gain when he said, "instead of focusing on how to build the good initiatives of their predecessors, governments sometimes spend half of their terms to dismantle the work of their predecessors, with the intention of making them unpopular." This call is appropriate and direct to African leaders rather to concentrate on helping one another to propel the continent to prosperity. All the parties after the election should work together for the good of the people and their nation's development but this seem to be a mirage in many African nations.

Today, the problems in Africa keep on mounting and as I stated before we need people who are committed and ready to lead the continent by changing the attitude of the people, empowering them and injecting them with a sense of urgency to do something to change the face of Africa. Such leaders should have the qualities that we enumerated before and should dedicate their lives for the service of the African people, otherwise the same problem will recycle itself and Africa will never see progress. Such leadership should begin from the basic levels, the grassroots. The people attain leadership positions in these levels not to lord it over the people but to mobilize them for effective work. I would suggest that this begins from the rural areas where the leadership has many possibilities to introduce change. The leader works with the people to bring in electricity since in this modern time solar energy does not need the extension of power lines from far away; or new and affordable ways of providing energy could be sourced for development; the used of potable water is something that could be thought of and provided to the people. This involves creating water systems from what is locally available. The leaders should help the people to think of what resources they have locally and what can be done to harness these local resources for their betterment. We can go on and on but the crux of the matter is that the people need a leader who will ask insightful questions pertaining to the environment and the needs of the people and try to find solutions. God has given every human being the ability to master their environment and improve on what God has given them. I wonder how people in snow falling regions have been able to protect themselves from the killing cold. They have to think and do something and the next generations have to build on what their ancestors left behind and that goes on and on. In Europe where I lived lots of people have solar panels on their roofs to capture even the little sun they get and sell the excess to get some money. It is an investment and also a business. Africa has a lot of sun shining many hours a day and the people only complain about the heat. How can the energy be used even to provide affordable air-conditioners for many homes against the heat? I believe that leadership at the basic level can do something to change the lives of the people. This may not be easy but there is an educated person coming from each village who does not only go to the village to show off his or her riches from the cities but to be an agent of change in the village. This is where the chiefs also come in to identify and appeal to these people to help them realize something positive for the people.

The political parties are also broad-based and have their presence in every corner of the nation. This is because they need the votes of the people to come into power. During electioneering campaigns they promise the people so many things and even use money and goods to influence the conscience of the people. In many instances therefore elections are not won on someone's vision, ideologies and conviction but because of what one receives from a politician. It is sad to state that after the politicians have come into power they renegade on their promises but have no shame to come back again during the next elections to campaign and again offer monies, goods and promises for votes. In Ghana, for instance, some politicians are of the view that campaign promises are part of the elections and they are not met to be kept and so the people should rather hold their politicians on their manifestoes. But I think to promise someone is to make a commitment to do something for the person and I think this is legally binding and should be kept and fulfilled. After all can a written word read by itself? It has to be spoken. What the people promise are also written down either on paper or on the tablet of the hearts of the people. Politicians should therefore not deceive themselves when they go about making campaign promises. The people of Africa should be bold and hold them responsible to their promises.

It is sad to read that some African politicians result to juju to win power and influence. The result of this is the killing of innocent power for the preparation of this juju. It is no wonder that such belief and practice seem widespread. In Ghana, the Asantehene, Otumfuo Osei Tutu II, came out publicly to condemn such practices. If that is the case then one can easily deduce the reason why such people seek power. It is not for the good of the people but their own selfish ends and this does no good to the nation or the continent.

The magnitude of the problems in Africa calls for leaders who can adapt their leadership style to the prevailing conditions in Africa. Since many people are of the view that leadership is a problem in Africa, it means that the people really want a change from their situation but they also need someone with a vision and direction who will mobilize them to reach their goal. Such leaders should be strong, focused and not to give in to any distraction since there are a few people who would find it difficult to part from their corrupt ways and practices and pose hindrance to anything that would cut their sources of finance and influence. Leaders of course are to weather the challenges that confront them with calmness and determined on the course for change.

Africa should move away from the situation where politicians feed on the ignorance of the people. But it is also important for the people to inform themselves on issues and the people they want to vote for and make the right decision and choice of their leaders for the betterment of their lives. It is also important to hold their leaders accountable and use their thumb to show them the exit if they do not work on their behalf. This sense of awareness will help them come of their poverty and depravation.

The religious leaders have a great role to play in Africa's leadership structure. They have the ears of the people every day and weekends and can use the pulpit to give messages that are enlivened and holistically beneficial to the people. We saw this in the civil rights movements of Dr. Martin Luther King Jnr. The question that preachers should ask themselves is, what situation do the people find themselves in today? What are their needs, their fears and aspiration? how can the Gospel be used to address the needs of the people? Which is the right way to go to respond to the needs of the people? The actions that religious leaders may take would lead to stepping on the toes of some people but they should take strength from Jesus Christ who opted for the poor and sought for their wellbeing and betterment in the society in spite of trials and persecution. In doing this the rich and influential should also not be forgotten since some of them may need direction as to how to help the poor and the need in the society and uplift their lives. There is no need for people to be worried or have fears if the situation is good for all and we all enjoy the good things of this earth. Such a mindset will really bring Africa out of many problems and the saying that it is now time for Africa will make sense and a reality.

7.6 Recommendations

Africa needs good and effective leaders. For this to happen we need to give the youth a formation in leadership. This can be done by establishing youth leadership training centres where the youth receive a well structured and tailored instruction on leadership based on the needs of the particular nation. This should not be turned into youth ideological training centre for a particular party.

The youth should also be trained for leadership in their various societies. This can be in the scout, the youth societies in the religious organizations and in the various clubs in towns and villages. A course on leadership should also feature in the curricula of schools in Africa. I am of the view that if leadership is our weakness then we should invest in it and train people for it. It may need some time and money but the end result will be great. It is also very important that chiefs do not only accrue to themselves royalties and live extravagant lifestyles. Chiefs and queens should help drive their people into a new level and make sure that they work in unison with the local political and religious authorities for a better community. It is when the rural areas are developed that the youth people remain and help in their further development, otherwise they will all run away to the cities. There are also many places where they could source for funds to develop their areas but it is important that the people also organize something so that others will come and help, for God helps those who help themselves.

We should also understand that leadership is a gratuitous gift of God. Leaders should not lose that consciousness that they are given this singular opportunity to be leaders no to lord it over the people but to be their servants. In this way they think of the people before they think of themselves. Such knowledge will help leaders not to be greedy and corrupt but to serve the interest of the people. Also, the people who are led should be able to put the leaders on their toes and let them function. This should not be done through insults and undermining acts but using the institutions of state to address incompetency and abuse of power. The people have a role to play in making leaders what they become. The people should think of their themselves and their future, their village, the next generation to come before they the pittance they receive from unscrupulous politicians to make inform decision so that do not put themselves into perpetual hardship.

It is my ardent hope that when some of these suggestions are taken and put in action many of the problems in Africa would be solved.

7.7 Conclusions

In conclusion, it would be important to state that getting the right leader is not easy, especially in a situation where self-interest is exhibited with impunity; and the lackadaisical behavior of some people because of being disappointed in leadership or because of what they receive for keeping them quite. In any case the repercussion is the suffering of many African people. I have tried to give some suggestions as to what can be done to build up leadership for African nations which will eventually build up the entire continent. The problem is that many Africans do not read to inform themselves. Those who try to read should share what they read with their neighbors. The popular saying that if you want to hide something from the African put it in a book is true to some extent as the reading culture is very low. But we have to work hard to dismiss this assertion. There is hope for Africa and Africans should give the green light that they are prepared to play their part in moving the world forward.

AFRICA

Africa, the amazing continent,
Lying gorgeously on the belly of the earth,
Basking in the glow of the sun,
Bequeathed with abundant wealth.

Africa, a continent rich in eatables and drinkables,
Wonderful and beautiful People, beautiful animals,
birds and insects,
Whose habitation in Africa is a delight to behold.
The cacophonous harmony of the roaring sea, the
silent whispers of the rivers, the lakes and the
lagoons; and the mighty trees adorn your elegance.

From the coastland through to the forest and
Savanna, to the desert regions,
Africa, like the colors of the peacock, dazzles the
world with her beauty and magnificence.

Africa, a continent of tradition and culture,
Intelligence, bravery and hospitality.
You have been shattered by historical events,
The tides seem to turn against you,
The currents seem to upset you,
But you are not vanquished.

Instead of living in peace and tranquility,
Your people are fighting each other,

Your people are hungry, thirsty and depressed,
Your people are running away for greener pastures,
To the lands unlike Africa.
Problems compound each day,
Equity, justice, righteousness and charity cry out.

For the sake of Mother Africa,
Blow the dirt off each other's eyes
Master nature as our fathers and mothers taught us.
Take hold of your destiny and build up for
tomorrow's generation.

Hold yourselves in high esteem in the world,
Unite and show to the world that, there is hope for
Africa.
Africa, the continent of the Sun,
The Sun will shine on Africa.

Africa's renaissance now!

Bibliography

Books and Articles from Journal

Avgerou, C. (2001) "The Significance of Context in Information Systems and Organisational Change", *Information Systems Journal*, 11, London 2001.

Björn-Sören Gigler , "Barriers to ICTs for the Poor", in: Food and Agriculture Organization of the United Nations, Ninth United Nations Roundtable on Communication for Development, 2004 Rome.

Dagron, A G., Making Waves: Stories of Participatory Communication for Social Change, New York 2001.

Flannery, A., (ed.), "Decree on Apostolate to Lay People" in: Vatican Council II Documents, Vol. 1., The Conciliar and Post Conciliar Documents, Northport, New York 1982.

Lakoff, S. A., Democracy: History, Theory and Practice, Boulder, Co 1996.

Ogbodah, C., Democratization and the media in West Africa: *An Analysis Of* Recent Constitutional And Legislative Reforms For Press Freedom In Ghana and Nigeria, *West Africa* Review, no. 6 *2004.*

Panos Report, Women's health: Using Human
Rights to regain Reproductive Rights, Panos
Briefing, no. 32 London.

Richard Gunther & Mughan Anthony, Democracy
and the Media, A Comparative Perspective,
Cambidge 2000.

Sarpong, P. K., Ghana in Retrospect, Accra 1974.

The Economist, "Africa, the Hopeless Continent?",
in: London May 13-19, 2000 edition.

Torero, M., and Von Braun, J., (eds.), Information
and Communication Technologies for
Development and Poverty Reduction: The
Potential of Telecommunications
(International Food Policy Research
Institute), Baltimore 2006.

Walsham, G., Interpreting Informationn System in
an Organizations, Chichester: Wiley 1993.

Wiafe, E. O., The Rescue; Essayys on Topical Issues
for Ghanaian Christians, Accra 2004.

Internet Sources

Annan, K., Kofi Annan slams "PHD" Politics, in:
http://news.myjoyonline.com/politics/201010
/54537.asp, 08.12.2010.

Hamelink, C. J., New Information and
Communication technologies, Social
Development and Cultural Change,
UNRISD   Discussion Paper, June 1997,
in:
www.**unrisd**.org/80256B3C005BCCF9/(http
AuxPages)/.../dp86.pdf, 06.12.2010.

Merriam-Webster, Information, in:
http://www.merriam-webster.com/,
06.12.2020.

Wade, R. H., Globalisation, Poverty and Income
Distribution: Does the Liberal Argument
hold? 2002. in:
http://www.rba.gov.au/publications/confs/20
02/wade.pdf

Other Books by the Author:

Rev. Fr. Dr. **Eric Kwabena Oduro Wiafe**

Title: **Inter-religious Dialogue and Cooperation among the three Major Religions of Ghana**

Project Summary:

In Africa, there is a growing awareness, even among scholars, that there have not been much constructive dialogue between Christianity, African traditional Religion (ATR) and Islam. But such Inter-religious dialogue is necessary for peace in the world as religion holds a major place in fostering social integration, mutual understanding and peaceful convivance. Religion also serves as a catalyst for world peace. The study examines the case of Inter-religious dialogue in Ghana and the efforts being made to encourage adherents of the different religious groups to engage in Inter-religious dialogue and Cooperation as a way of demolishing the walls of prejudice stone by stone and build bridges of dialogue rather than erect barriers of hatred, vengeance and hostility (Cfr. Hans Küng, 2007). Ghana is a democratic and relatively stable and peaceful country, but there have been cases of religiously motivated violence and so in order to bring peace and understanding there is the necessity for Inter-religious dialogue.

Religion influences the daily lives and activities of the people in Ghana in a significant way. Therefore, the study looks at two major belief systems and practices in Ghana, namely, witchcraft, which has led to the establishment of the witchcraft colony in Gambaga among others, and the belief and practice of Trokosi, which is a practice whereby a family gives out a girl-child to the traditional shrine to serve there for a period of time as a reparation due to an offence committed by a member of her family. We examined how through Inter-religious dialogue such beliefs and practices could be handled and consensus built up for peaceful living together. This is based on the truism that, in a society, where there exist various religious groups, like in the case of Ghana, constructive dialogue can help the people find solutions to major challenges confronting them, which otherwise may lead to violence and instability. In this study therefore, the necessity of inter-religious dialogue for Ghana becomes a Sine qua non to explore ways and means to overcome prejudice, to live and work together for peace and progress in Ghana.

Language: English
Year of Publication: 2010
Number of pages: 190
ISBN: 978-3-86624-498-6
PREMIUM
Publisher: dissertation.de - Verlag im Internet GmbH
Book Price: 43.50 EUR
PDF-Price: 25.88 EUR

Book found in:

a. http://www.amazon.de/Inter-religious-dialogue-among-three-religions/dp/3866244983/ref=sr_1_1?ie=UTF8&s=books-intl-de&qid=1291759824&sr=8-1
b. http://www.dissertation.de/buch.php3?buch=6120

Title: The three major Religions in Ghana: History, Theology and Influence

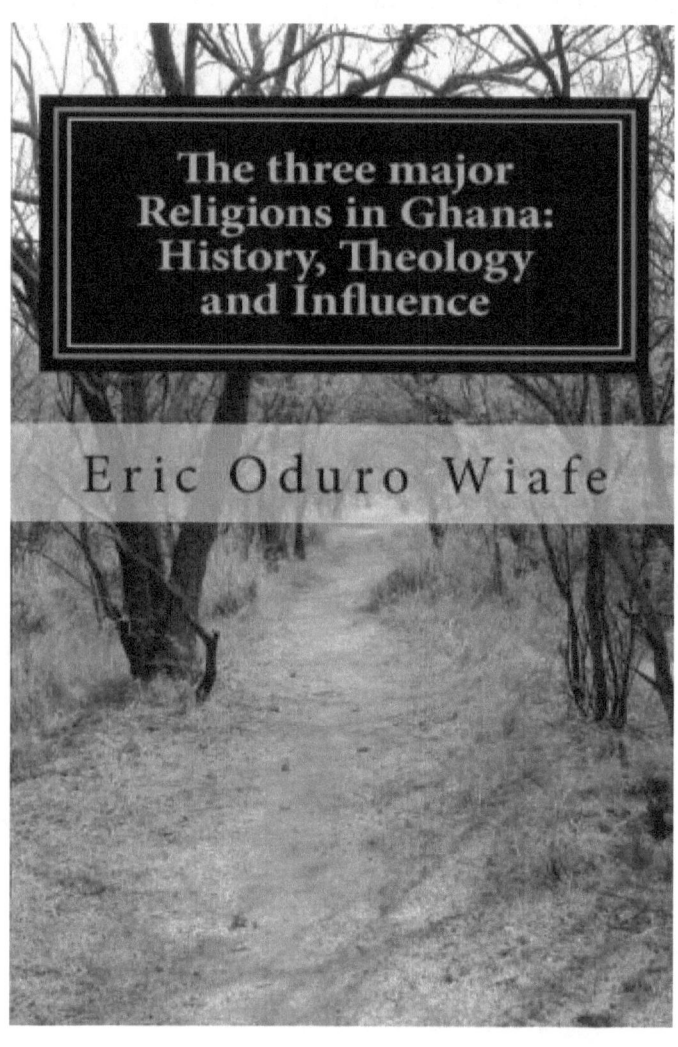

The three major
Religions in Ghana:
History, Theology
and Influence

Eric Oduro Wiafe

Project Summary:

African Traditional Religion, Christianity and Islam are the three major religious groups in Ghana. They play a prominent and significant role in the holistic life of Ghanaians from the political, economical, educational, religious and the family. This experience is not only limited to Ghana but the entire African continent.

The purpose of this book is to help people not only to know about their religious faith but also the religious faith of their neighbors so that they can live in mutual respect, peace and convivance.

List Price: $29.99
6" x 9"   (15.24 x 22.86 cm)
Number of pages: 176
ISBN-13:   978-1456350581
ISBN-10:   1456350587

Book Found in:

a. https://www.createspace.com/3498839
b. http://www.amazon.de/s/ref=nb_sb_noss?_
   mk_de_DE=%C5M%C5Z%D5%D1&url=se
   arch-alias%3Daps&field-
   keywords=eric+wiafe&x=0&y=0

Title: The Role of Religion in Poverty Alleviation in Africa

Project Summary:

114

Is Africa a poor continent, a continent without hope? The answer is straightforward and definitely NO. Africa is not poor. The people are also not poor but they have been made poor by a multiplicity of factors. Africa as a continent is potentially endowed with rich natural and human resources. The question now is how the continent is working out of poverty so that the people experience, at least, some concrete glimpses of riches in their daily lives?

Also, it is a truism that Africans are religious and today the major religions in Africa are impacting on the lives of the people in a significant way from cradle to grave. On the one hand religion can be said to be helping in ameliorating poverty and on the other hand, it is used as an instrument of deepening the poverty status of the people. This places religion at the centre of both Africa's development and poverty. The writer therefore touches on the understanding of the three major religions in Africa of poverty and how the religious groups are trying to deal with this phenomenon of poverty. It is the hope that many people will gain from this work and contribute their quota to Africa's Renaissance.

List Price: $39.99
6" x 9"   (15.24 x 22.86 cm)
Number of pages: 204
ISBN-13: 978-1456367190
ISBN-10: 1456367196

Book found in:

a. https://www.createspace.com/3505215
b. http://www.amazon.de/s/ref=nb_sb_noss?_mk_de_DE=%C5M%C5Z%D5%D1&url=search-alias%3Daps&field-keywords=eric+wiafe&x=0&y=0

Title: Christianity and African Traditional Religion's Approach to issues of Life and Death

Project Summary:

This study is concerned with the response that the Catholic Church, specifically the Catholic Archdiocese of Accra, is giving to the Akan traditional concept of life and death. The focus group is the Akan of the Catholic Archdiocese of Accra.

The research revealed the difficult situation of Akan

117

Catholics in the face of their Akan traditional practice. In some situations Akan Catholics have to make a choice between their Roman Catholic practice and their Akan traditional practice. An example is whether to go through the widowhood rites as required by Akan tradition or not. We also found in the research the importance that the Catholic Church, and for that matter the Catholic Archdiocese of Accra in particular, is giving to all these situations so as to help the people to conform to the beliefs and practices of the Church. This indicates the seriousness that the Church attaches to inculturation. The Church does not want to make the mistake of the past where some missionaries condemned everything African and tried to westernize Africans through religion. The Church acknowledges that the key to the growth and future of the Church in Africa is inculturation. In quoting Platvoet, Omenyo states that the Akan Traditional Religion is very accommodating, adaptable and highly dynamic (Omenyo, C. N., 2002). The Catholic Church, therefore, has to study the Akan traditional religion and explore all the possibilities to inculturate some of the beliefs and practices of Akan traditional religion so as to enhance her evangelizing mission.

In view of the above, this work attests to the responses that the Church has given to the various issues that were raised in the discussions, namely the issues of life and death.

118

The Church is doing something concrete on making Akan Catholics understand their faith and live by it. This becomes imperative when it comes to the issue of childbearing. On this issue Akans see barrenness as a problem, and so they are taught by the clergy and their lay collaborators the reasons for barrenness and the need to accept the will of God in their lives.

On the subject of death, the response of the Roman Catholic Church is mainly in teaching on the need for Christians to believe in the resurrection of Jesus Christ. The Catholic Archdiocese of Accra is responding to the various traditional death and funeral rituals, especially widowhood rites, and putting in place an alternative for Catholics in the Archdiocese of Accra. This is saving many women from the rigorous and inhuman treatment of widows(ers).

The response of the Church makes her teachings and beliefs more meaningful and acceptable and thus enhances the Church's *growth in all aspects of her life.*

Year of Publication: 2010
Number of pages: 176
ISBN: 978-3-86624-512-9
PREMIUM
Publisher: dissertation.de - Verlag im Internet GmbH
Book Price: 43.90 EUR

PDF-Price: 26.12 EUR

Book found in:

1. http://www.dissertation.de/index.php3?active
   _document=buch.php3&sprache=2&buch=6
   137

Summary of pages where one can order these books:

a. https://www.createspace.com/3498839
b. https://www.createspace.com/3505215
c. http://www.amazon.de/s/ref=nb_sb_noss?
   mk_de_DE=%C5M%C5Z%D5%D1&url=se
   arch-alias%3Daps&field-
   keywords=eric+wiafe&x=0&y=0
d. http://www.dissertation.de/index.php3?active
   _document=buch.php3&sprache=2&buch=6
   137

Contact E-Mail address of Author, Rev. Fr. Dr. Eric
Oduro Wiafe is, frekow5@yahoo.com